US SEVENTH FLEET, VIETNAM 1964–75

American naval power in Southeast Asia

Edward J. Marolda
Illustrated by Adam Tooby

OSPREY PUBLISHING
Bloomsbury Publishing Plc
Kemp House, Chawley Park, Cumnor Hill, Oxford OX2 9PH, UK
29 Earlsfort Terrace, Dublin 2, Ireland
1385 Broadway, 5th Floor, New York, NY 10018, USA
E-mail: info@ospreypublishing.com
www.ospreypublishing.com

OSPREY is a trademark of Osprey Publishing Ltd

First published in Great Britain in 2023

A catalog record for this book is available from the British Library.

ISBN: PB 9781472856814; eBook 9781472856807; ePDF 9781472856821; XML 9781472856791

23 24 25 26 27   10 9 8 7 6 5 4 3 2 1

Maps by bounford.com
Diagrams by Adam Tooby
Battlescenes by Adam Tooby
Index by Janet Andrew
Typeset by Myriam Bell Design
Printed and bound in India by Replika Press Private Ltd.

Front Cover: Art by Adam Tooby, © Osprey Publishing

Osprey Publishing supports the Woodland Trust, the UK's leading woodland conservation charity.

To find out more about our authors and books visit www.ospreypublishing.com. Here you will find
extracts, author interviews, details of forthcoming events and the option to sign up for our newsletter.

CONTENTS

THE FLEET'S PURPOSE

The US Seventh Fleet, the combat-hardened naval arm of General Douglas MacArthur's Southwest Pacific command in World War II, made its Cold War debut transporting US Army troops of the XXIV Corps to Korea in September 1945. It became a primary military instrument of US foreign policy in the region during and after the First Indochina War (1946–54), fought by colonial France. Having departed its base at Qingdao, China, in 1949, the Seventh Fleet was now based at Subic Bay in the newly independent Republic of the Philippines. It was responsible for deterring hostile activity against America's allies and interests and, from 1959 through 1962, the fleet deployed on numerous occasions to waters off Indochina as a demonstration of US resolve to oppose Communist inroads in Laos.

The Seventh Fleet's Cold War mission evolved in 1964 from peacetime deterrence and maritime presence to the employment of naval combat power in support of US grand strategy and foreign policy. Frustrated with the disorder in the political and security situation in the Republic of Vietnam (RVN) after President Ngo Dinh Diem's assassination in November 1963, new President Lyndon B. Johnson and his defense secretary, Robert S. McNamara, used the Military Assistance Command, Vietnam (MACV) and the Seventh Fleet in a major effort to discourage Hanoi's support for the Communist insurgencies in Indochina. Super-secret organizations in Washington and Saigon had earlier established a naval unit whose mission, in Operation *34A*, was to bring the conflict to North Vietnam. MACV's Studies and Observations Group ran the program. The US Navy supplied Norwegian-built fast patrol boats (PTFs), trained the Vietnamese crews, and maintained the vessels at a base in Danang, South Vietnam. The PTFs, called "Nastys," were armed with 40mm and 20mm guns, 81mm mortars, .50-caliber machine guns, and recoilless rifles. The unit landed saboteurs early in 1964 who attempted – but mostly failed – to blow up military targets ashore. The *34A* unit then switched in early

August to hit-and-run, nighttime bombardments against sites on the coast and on offshore islands.

Washington also directed Seventh Fleet destroyers, in the longtime Desoto Patrol program, to carry out intelligence-collection missions along the coast of North Vietnam. Unlike previous operations far from the coasts of China, the Soviet Union, North Korea, and North Vietnam, this time the ships were ordered to steam as close as 8 miles from North Vietnam and 4 miles from its offshore islands. The proximity of these patrols to North Vietnam was meant as one more signal of Washington's displeasure with Hanoi's actions in Indochina. To the surprise of President Johnson and his civilian and military advisors, the North Vietnamese came out fighting. On the afternoon of August 2, 1964, a trio of Soviet-built P-4 torpedo boats crewed by 11 sailors, capable of 52-knot speeds, and armed with torpedoes and 14.5mm guns, closed with destroyer *Maddox* (DD-731). The P-4s of Section 3, PT Squadron 135 launched their six torpedoes at the American ship but missed, and then opened up with their deck guns. One round lodged in the destroyer's superstructure. Return fire from *Maddox* failed to discourage the attackers and probably failed to hit any of the boats, but 20mm cannon and Zuni rocket fire from four *Ticonderoga* (CVA-14) F-8 Crusader fighters, which arrived overhead during the battle, killed the captain of one of the PT boats and left another boat dead in the water. Later Medal of Honor recipient and vice-presidential contender James B. Stockdale piloted one of the F-8s. Despite the American attack, all three of the North Vietnamese boats eventually reached shore to fight another day.

Johnson and his civilian advisors in Washington and the top commanders in the Far East, Admiral Ulysses S. G. Sharp, Commander in Chief, Pacific, and Admiral Thomas H. Moorer, Commander in Chief, US Pacific Fleet, were of one mind that North Vietnam's daylight attack on the US Navy could not go unpunished lest the military pressure campaign lose credibility. At the time, it was universally accepted by America's national security establishment that

Aircraft carrier *Tarawa* (CV-40) and light cruiser *Tucson* (CL-98), anchored off Qingdao (Tsingtao), homeport of the US Seventh Fleet in China from 1946 to 1949. During the post-World War II era, the fleet's primary mission was to deter potential adversaries and protect US interests in the Western Pacific. (NHHC)

North Vietnam had neither the capability nor the will to fight the United States. Secretary of the Navy Paul Nitze was not alone in assuming that US air and naval power "would favor the United States so greatly that regardless of what North Vietnam did we would prevail in a comparably short period of time."

Washington ordered *Maddox*, joined by Forrest Sherman-class destroyer *Turner Joy* (DD-951), to continue the coastal patrol. Moorer, the Seventh Fleet commander only two months before, told his successor, Vice Admiral Roy Johnson, that the destroyers should spend the next four days operating around the Hon Me island hot spot – essentially an "in your face" action. On the night of August 4, far out in the gulf, the ships reported that they were under another North Vietnamese torpedo attack, an assertion initially supported by National Security Agency (NSA) analysts. The Navy's and the NSA's reports, however, were in error. US intelligence later determined that there was no attack on the destroyers that night.

Convinced, however, in the heat of the moment that these ships had been the victims of another North Vietnamese naval action, the president ordered a two-carrier, multiplane retaliatory strike on Hanoi's naval forces and the petroleum storage facility at Vinh. On August 5, in Operation *Pierce Arrow*, the *Ticonderoga* and *Constellation* (CVA-64) air wings executed 64 sorties against Vinh and enemy naval vessels at Quang Khe, Hon Gai, and in the Lach Truong/ Hon Ne area. The US naval aviators strafed and rocketed around two dozen enemy boats and sank some of them. North Vietnamese antiaircraft gunners shot down the A-4C Skyhawk of Lieutenant (jg) Everett Alvarez Jr, who spent the next eight and a half years in captivity, and the A-1 Skyraider of pilot Richard C. Sather, who was killed.

With combat having now been joined between the regular naval forces of the United States and North Vietnam, on August 7 President Johnson asked for and Congress approved what came to be known as the Gulf of Tonkin Resolution. The pronouncement enabled the president to employ the American armed forces in defense of the non-Communist nations of Indochina and would serve as the legal underpinning of the US war effort from 1964 to 1971, when it was repealed.

SEVENTH FLEET AT THE DAWN OF WAR

Washington continued to give lip service to the administration's policy of military pressure against North Vietnam after the Tonkin Gulf incident, but despite the pleas of admirals Sharp and Moorer that effort fizzled. Washington canceled or postponed most of the *34A* maritime operations on North Vietnam's coast for the remainder of 1964. Seventh Fleet destroyers *Morton* (DD-948) and *Richard S. Edwards* (DD-950) carried out a Desoto Patrol mission in the gulf on September 17–18, but US leaders kept the warships well away from North Vietnam and it proved to be the last such operation.

Ngo Dinh Diem, President of the Republic of Vietnam from 1955 to 1963, speaks to sailors of the new South Vietnamese navy. The men would soon shed their French-influenced uniforms in favor of US Navy whites, a reflection of Diem's anti-French inclination and increasing reliance on the United States. (NHHC)

While Hanoi went on the offensive against South Vietnam, convinced the United States would not invade or bomb it into oblivion, Washington relied on the political science theory of "graduated escalation." The Seventh Fleet and the Seventh Air Force were tasked with the execution of that strategic approach. In December 1964, carrier- and shore-based aircraft began bombing selected Communist military targets on the Ho Chi Minh Trail and in central Laos. A key goal was to convince Hanoi that its behavior risked even greater US military intervention. The fleet's first mission in Operation *Barrel Roll* involved four A-1H Skyraider attack planes flying from carrier *Ranger* (CVA-61) that destroyed only a few buildings and failed to drop a bridge. The Navy and the Air Force carried out similar strikes in the following months with much the same result. Eventually, US leaders came to doubt that the North Vietnamese even recognized these pinprick actions as an increase in military pressure.

Undeterred by US actions, on February 7, 1965 Communist forces shelled a US advisors' barracks in Pleiku, South Vietnam, causing more than 100 American casualties. Washington responded in kind. The president authorized a one-time, tit-for-tat operation by Seventh Fleet, US Air Force, and Vietnam Air Force (VNAF) planes. The Navy's strike in Operation *Flaming Dart* hit the barracks of the North Vietnamese 325th Division at Dong Hoi, just north of the demilitarized zone. The Seventh Fleet attackers destroyed or damaged only 22 of the 275 buildings at the site. Unfazed by the retaliatory action, three days later Viet Cong guerrillas killed more American military personnel at a barracks in Qui Nhon, South Vietnam. The US reaction to this attack involved a 99-plane strike by *Ranger*, *Coral Sea* (CVA-43), and *Hancock* (CVA-19) on the North Vietnamese barracks at Chanh Hoa that flattened a few more buildings. There was no discernable change to enemy behavior.

The Seventh Fleet's Attack Carrier Striking Force (Task Force 77) underway in the Gulf of Tonkin. Trailing *Constellation* are carrier *Oriskany* (CVA-34), destroyers *George K. MacKenzie* (DD-836) and *Rogers* (DD-876), and ammunition ship *Mount Katmai* (AE-16). Different destroyer types protected the carriers from surface, air, and submarine attack and logistic vessels such as *Mount Katmai* kept the naval force well supplied with fuel, ammunition, and consumables. During the war, three or four carriers, several cruisers, and 20 destroyer types routinely steamed with Task Force 77. (NHHC)

A PLANNED CAMPAIGN OF *ROLLING THUNDER*

In keeping with the graduated escalation approach, the Johnson administration then suggested that only a heavy, sustained bombing campaign against North Vietnam had the potential to change the course of the war. The president and his advisors sought to convince the leaders in Hanoi that their quest for a united Vietnam could only end in failure. The American leaders concluded that the United States could achieve its goals without resorting to all-out war or triggering Chinese or Soviet intervention on the side of North Vietnam. Indeed, the specter of Mao Zedong's People's Liberation Army storming into the Tonkin Delta to support fellow Marxist-Leninists – a real threat – kept President Johnson awake at night and eventually hampered the Seventh Fleet's execution of operations.

Even as Operation *Rolling Thunder* got underway in March 1965, President Johnson made a change to the US strategy that seriously complicated the Seventh Fleet's mission. The new strategic approach focused not on compelling North Vietnam's leaders to give up their quest for a united Vietnam but using US military power to prevent that from happening. The object was not to win the war but prevent a defeat. The muscle behind that strategy was the deployment to South Vietnam beginning in March 1965 of what ultimately became a half-million-strong expeditionary force. To support the ground war in Indochina, the Seventh Fleet's air and surface operations after 1965 increasingly concentrated on interdicting seaborne infiltration, logistic traffic on the Ho Chi Minh Trail, and combat support to allied ground forces in South Vietnam, Laos, and Cambodia. At the same time, the fleet had to devote major resources to the agonizingly slow, costly, and indecisive *Rolling Thunder* bombing campaign against North Vietnam.

FLEET FIGHTING POWER

NAVAL AVIATION

The Seventh Fleet's most lethal component, its Attack Carrier Striking Force (Task Force 77), brought heavy combat power and capability to the operational theater. The 59,650-long-ton (79,000 fully loaded), 1,039ft *Forrestal* (CVA-9) and the three other ships of that class reflected many of the post-World War II design features incorporated in what was to have been the first of the Navy's "supercarriers," *United States* (CVA-58), canceled by the Truman administration in 1949. The Korean War experience highlighted the need for larger, more hardened flight decks capable of handling jet aircraft and more sizable air wings for operations against shore targets. Improvements over previous ship types included armored and angled flight decks, four steam catapults, the Fresnel Lens Visual Landing Air system, and four elevators to speed the movement of planes from the hangar deck to the flight deck. The Kitty Hawk class, similar in many ways to the Forrestal class, boasted RIM-2 Terrier surface-to-air missile systems and reconfigured flight decks that increased the efficiency and safety of launch and recovery operations. Both classes were built to accommodate heavy, nuclear-capable bombers but the advent in the late 1950s of miniaturized "nukes" and smaller aircraft freed up space for more attack planes and fighters. The Forrestal-class ships carried 750,000 gallons of fuel for their aircraft. To better support air operations, the Navy reconfigured the Kitty Hawk-class ships to hold 1,900,000 gallons of aviation fuel. Both classes accommodated more than 80 aircraft and 2,000 tons of ordnance. The Forrestal- and Kitty Hawk-class ships operated eight Babcock and Wilcox boilers and four Westinghouse geared turbine engines that generated 260,000 (280,000 for the Kitty Hawks) shaft horsepower (shp) that drove four propellers and enabled the ships to reach 33–35 knots at top speed. The personnel complement for each of the Forrestal and Kitty Hawk ships included 2,750 officer and enlisted sailors to run the ship and 2,150 aircrew and other men to operate the air wing.

When *Enterprise* (CVAN-65), the Navy's first nuclear-powered aircraft carrier, joined the fight off Vietnam in December 1965, this carrier brought to the fleet a ship of unprecedented capability. Indeed, on the carrier's combat debut in Vietnam, *Enterprise*'s Carrier Air Wing 9 set a record of 165 strike sorties in a single day. The 94,700-ton carrier was powered by eight nuclear reactors able to propel the ship at 33 knots and operate for years without refueling. Freed from that need, the carrier could hold huge stores of aviation fuel (2,800,000 gallons) and ordnance and operate independently of slower oilers and ammunition ships. The ship's crew and air wing totaled more than 5,000 men. The long, 1,079ft flight deck and spacious hangar decks enabled the ship to accommodate up to 90 aircraft grouped in two F-4B Phantom and four A-4C Skyhawk squadrons, in addition to aerial tankers, photo reconnaissance and electronic countermeasures aircraft, and helicopters.

While less capable in some ways than the supercarriers, the 27,000-long-ton, 862ft Essex-class and 45,000-long-ton, 972ft Midway-class ships built in World War II or just afterward proved to be valuable Cold War resources. In the carrier modernization projects 27A and 27C of the 1950s, the Navy strengthened flight decks, added optical landing systems, increased elevator and fuel storage capabilities, and installed hydraulic and later steam-powered catapults with blast deflectors. Another major innovation was the angled flight deck that optimized flight deck space. During the late 1950s and early 1960s, a number of the Essex-class ships served as antisubmarine warfare carriers with the CVS designation. The three Midways operated as full-fledged attack carriers. As the number of more modern Forrestal-class carriers and larger aircraft came on line during the war, the Navy retired many of the Essex-class ships.

For most of the war, the Task Force 77 carriers operated from a staging area known as Yankee Station (17° 30'N and 108° 30'E), located between the Chinese island of Hainan and the southern coast of North Vietnam. Task Force 77 carriers, three or four at a time, operated from Yankee Station. The air wings on each carrier, depending on the size of the ship, normally consisted of two fighter and three attack squadrons and smaller detachments of helicopters and air early warning, refueling, and electronic countermeasures aircraft.

The attack aircraft squadrons employed A-4 Skyhawks, A-7 Corsairs, F-4 Phantoms, all-weather, day-night A-6 Intruders, and propeller-driven A-1 Skyraiders. The two heavyweights of the fighter community were the F-4 Phantoms armed with air-to-air missiles and the F-8 Crusaders armed with both missiles and 20mm guns. Accomplishing most of the aerial reconnaissance missions were RA-5C Vigilantes and RA-3B Skywarriors. Electronic countermeasures tasks were carried out by Skyraider, Skywarrior, and Intruder variants and later in the war EA-6B Prowlers. Grumman E-2 Hawkeyes warned strike aircraft of approaching MiGs, guided them to and from their targets ashore, and facilitated communications.

Attack and fighter aircraft employed a range of ordnance from Korean War-era "dumb bombs" to advanced missiles and precision-guided munitions. Attack aircraft dropped 250, 500, 1,000, and 2,000lb general purpose bombs in the operations in North Vietnam, Laos, and South Vietnam, and also napalm bombs in the south. Later in the war, carrier planes seeded rivers in North Vietnam with Mk-36 Destructor mines and the country's ports with several types of magnetic and acoustic sea mines. Attack aircraft also employed unguided 5in Zuni rockets, 2.75in rockets, Bullpup bombs, and Shrike anti-radar and Walleye TV-guided munitions against ground targets.

Complementing the Seventh Fleet's carrier force were its surface warships, including for a brief period the Iowa-class battleship *New Jersey* (BB-62) armed with 16in naval rifles. Guided missile destroyers, conventional destroyers, and destroyer escorts protected the carriers and the other ships of the fleet from air, surface, and sub-surface attack. Surface ships boasted Talos, Tartar, and Terrier surface-to-air missiles for defense against MiGs. Monitoring the air space over the fleet and over North Vietnam and Laos were nuclear-powered *Long Beach* (CGN-9), *Chicago* (CG-11), and other guided missile cruisers equipped with advanced air defense systems, such as the AN/SPS-32/33 fixed array radars. The ships operated from PIRAZ (positive identification radar advisory zone) stations in the northern gulf, routinely referred to as "Red Crown" for the mission's radio call sign. These ships worked to identify the hundreds of planes daily operating ashore and afloat: to determine if they were friend or foe; to warn US pilots of approaching MiGs or guide them to the enemy interceptors; to ensure that American pilots steered clear of Chinese air space; to aid in the coordination of search and rescue efforts; and to employ the cruisers' shipboard surface-to-air missiles to defend the fleet. These ships were normally paired with a conventional, gun-armed destroyer whose role was to protect the cruiser from an enemy torpedo boat attack.

The combat search and rescue (CSAR) responsibility was one of the fleet's most critical duties. The aviators and surface warriors of the Seventh Fleet understood that everything possible would be done to rescue aircrewmen whose

DAWN OF THE PGM ERA (overleaf)

This scene depicts the strike on October 6, 1972 by four Attack Squadron 82 ("Marauders") A-7E Corsairs (one piloted by later four-star Admiral Leighton W. "Snuffy" Smith) on the Thanh Hoa (Dragon's Jaw) Bridge. The bridge had withstood numerous attacks and kept on functioning during the *Rolling Thunder* and *Linebacker I* campaigns. This attack, which permanently severed the enemy's key transportation node, succeeded because of the use of Walleye ("Fat Albert") TV-guided air-to-surface, precision-guided munitions (PGM). This and other PGMs employed by the Navy and the Air Force changed the game, making

the *Linebacker* campaigns of 1972 operational successes and showed the promise of future air warfare.

In the cockpit, the pilot views a TV screen (which shows crosshairs on an image of the bridge) on his console as his Walleye detaches from the plane's starboard wing and heads for the target. His wingman's A-7 Corsair is shown on the port side of Smith's plane, simultaneously releasing its Walleye. Below, the other two A-7s on the mission are shown pulling out of their dive as their conventional bombs explode.

The 16in guns of *New Jersey* (BB-62), a veteran of World War II and the Korean War, shell enemy targets ashore. In Operation *Sea Dragon*, the battleship, along with numerous 8in- and 6in-gun cruisers and 5in-gun destroyers bombarded roads and railroads in southern North Vietnam and sank numerous coastal craft attempting to supply Communist forces in South Vietnam. (NHHC)

planes ended up in the Gulf of Tonkin or in the jungles of North Vietnam, Laos, or South Vietnam. On a rotating basis, destroyers were posted to a North SAR station (20°N and 107°E) and a South SAR station (19°N and 106°E). Sikorsky SH-3 Sea King and Kaman UH-2 Sea Sprite helicopters operating from the carriers or surface ships facilitated these rescue missions. The CSAR mission was truly a joint effort, with Air Force HU-16 Albatross amphibians, HH-3E "Jolly Green Giant" helicopters, and A-1 Skyraider attack planes based in Thailand and South Vietnam teaming up with the Navy. Operating at the North SAR station, the fleet's SAR Coordinator worked with on-scene commanders to provide Navy attack planes, kept on airborne standby, for the suppression of enemy ground fire during rescue missions.

THE SURFACE FLEET

In addition to the aircraft carriers and their air wings, the Seventh Fleet's primary means for bringing offensive power to bear against the enemy were surface warships armed with a powerful array of guns and missiles. In Operation *Sea Dragon*, a complement to *Rolling Thunder*'s air operations, heavy cruisers armed with 8in/55-caliber guns; guided missile light cruisers armed with 6in/47-caliber guns; destroyers armed with either 5in/54-caliber or 5in/38-caliber guns; and Royal Australian Navy destroyers bombarded bridges, rail lines, coastal craft, and enemy shore batteries. The fleet also had the capability with its Talos missiles to down enemy planes far inland and did so on several occasions during the war. During the *Linebacker* campaign of 1972, the fleet's cruisers and destroyers ranged the entire coast of North Vietnam complicating enemy efforts to supply forces in South Vietnam and shelling targets only miles from Haiphong and other ports.

Another responsibility of the Seventh Fleet's surface force was to assist American and allied forces battling Viet Cong and North Vietnamese forces in South Vietnam. The subordinate Naval Gunfire Support Unit of the Cruiser-Destroyer Group (TG 70.8) working with MACV, boasted cruisers, destroyers, medium rocket landing ships (LSMR), and an inshore fire support ship (IFS). The IFS and the LSMRs could fire 380 5in rockets simultaneously. The deep waters of the South China Sea enabled the guns of the larger ships to reach targets in one-third of northern South Vietnam and much of the coastal areas in central and southern South Vietnam.

AMPHIBIOUS CAPABILITIES

The fleet's Amphibious Task Force (Task Force 76) that provided the ships and Marines for the major amphibious landing operations in South Vietnam was heir to the legacy of the Marines and sailors who had stormed the beaches of Iwo Jima and Inchon. By the start of the Vietnam War, the Seventh Fleet's most versatile Navy–Marine combination was the Amphibious Ready Group/Special Landing Force (ARG/SLF). The ARG task group normally consisted of an amphibious assault ship (LPH), a dock landing ship (LSD), an attack transport (APA) or an amphibious transport dock (LPD), and a tank landing ship (LST). Organic to the Marine SLF task group and deployed on the LPH was a medium helicopter squadron equipped with 24 UH-34 Sea Horses. The ground combat element consisted of a 2,000-man

SURFACE SHIP CLASSES IN THE VIETNAM WAR	
Class	Number of Ships
Battleship and Cruisers	
Iowa-class BB	1
Baltimore-class CA/CAG	4
Cleveland-class CLG	4
Des Moines-class CA	1
Long Beach-class CGN	1
Guided Missile Destroyers	
Bainbridge-class DLGN	1
Truxton-class DLGN	1
Belknap-class DLG	9
Charles F. Adams-class DDG	15
Farragut-class DLG	7
Leahy-class DLG	7
Mitcher-class DDG	1
Destroyers	
Allen M. Sumner-class DD	34
Fletcher-class DD	30
Forrest Sherman-class DD	16
Gearing-class DD	87
Destroyer Escorts and Guided Missile Escorts	
Bronstein-class DE	1
Brooke-class DEG	3
Claud Jones-class DE	4
Courtney-class DE	4
Edsall-class DER	14
Garcia-class DE	5
Knox-class DE	19
Key BB: Battleship CA: Heavy cruiser CAG: Guided missile heavy cruiser CGN: Nuclear-powered cruiser CLG: Guided missile light cruiser DD: Destroyer DDG: Guided missile destroyer DE: Destroyer escort DEG: Guided missile ocean escort DER: Radar picket destroyer escort DLG: Destroyer leader DLGN: Nuclear-powered destroyer leader	

Amphibious assault ship *Iwo Jima* (LPH-2), landing ship dock *Thomaston* (LSD-28), and amphibious transport dock *Vancouver* (LPD-2) of the fleet's Amphibious Force (Task Force 76) steaming off the Mekong Delta during Operation *Deckhouse V* in January 1967. (NHHC)

Marines cross the flight deck of an amphibious assault ship to board UH-34 Sea Horse helicopters for Operation *Dagger Thrust* in central South Vietnam. The Fleet's Navy–Marine Amphibious Ready Group/Special Landing Force carried out 71 similar operations during the war. (NHHC)

infantry battalion landing team, reinforced with artillery, armor, engineer, and other support units. The men of these units and their equipment were divided among the ships of the ARG. Putting the troops on the beach was the responsibility of the helicopters and 41 organic tracked landing vehicles (LVT). Available for medical support were the Navy corpsmen and doctors serving with Marine units. Satisfying the demand for more amphibious capability, by the end of the war Task Force 76 employed three ARG/SLFs. With the exception of the large-scale Operation *Starlite* in August 1965 and *Jackstay* in the spring of 1966, most of the 69 operations conducted afterward entailed quick raids and sweeps in conjunction with US Army and Army of the Republic of Vietnam (ARVN) troops. The enemy's strong presence in northern South Vietnam, especially during the Tet Offensive, increasingly demanded the use of the ARG/SLF as an afloat reserve force and as reinforcement of the Marine units fighting desperately ashore.

SUBMARINES

Despite the absence of an undersea threat, the fleet's Submarine Group (Task Group 70. 9) did its part to support the war effort. Transport submarines *Perch* (APSS-312), *Tunny* (APSS-282), and *Grayback* (LPSS-574) put SEALs ashore in South Vietnam to reconnoiter prospective amphibious landing sites and carry out special operations. Attack submarines supported the *Market Time* anti-seaborne infiltration operation by trailing suspicious enemy trawlers and alerting the naval command in Saigon of an intruder's approach to South Vietnamese territorial waters.

In short, no other navy on earth equaled the enormous combat power and capability that the US Seventh Fleet brought to the fight off Vietnam.

HOW THE FLEET OPERATED

COMMAND AND CONTROL

The strategic and operational direction of the Seventh Fleet emanated from Washington and came down to the vice admiral in charge through a complex chain of command. President Johnson, Secretary of Defense McNamara, and other civilian advisors routinely gathered at the White House on Tuesdays for lunch to decide on *Rolling Thunder* bombing targets. They worked from data and plans drawn up by the Joint Chiefs of Staff (JCS) but were by no means tied to them. Not until October 1967 was the nation's top military leader, the chairman of the JCS, invited to attend the meeting. Once the president and his civilian advisors decided on bombing priorities, they were passed through the JCS to Commander in Chief, Pacific Command. Admiral Sharp worked with the commanders of his Navy and Air Force component commands, the Pacific Fleet and the Pacific Air Force, to improve the practicality and military effectiveness of those plans but he increasingly faced opposition from above. By the end of Sharp's tour in July 1968, President Johnson rarely took the advice of his commander of all US forces in the Pacific.

The four-star Commander in Chief, Pacific Command's (CINCPAC) naval component, and the immediate superior of the Seventh Fleet commander, was even less able to influence strategic and operational decisions, especially with regard to the bombing campaign. Admiral John Hyland, CINCPACFLT in the last year of *Rolling Thunder*, later admitted that "I really didn't have anything to say about what we were doing. Everything was decided in Washington, and then told to us." The Richard M. Nixon administration gave CINCPAC and the naval commands greater latitude in their conduct of operations, but still kept them on a tight leash with regard to bombing priorities and targets.

Further complicating the command and control of naval operations in Southeast Asia, Commander US Military Assistance Command, Vietnam (COMUSMACV), four-star Army generals William C. Westmoreland and after

CENTRALIZED COMMAND IN *ROLLING THUNDER*

From the outset of *Rolling Thunder*, Johnson and McNamara ordered extraordinary measures to avoid antagonizing Beijing or Moscow. The national command authority prohibited bombing operations within 30 nautical miles of China or Hanoi and 10 nautical miles of Haiphong. These early operational restrictions made many of North Vietnam's power plants, transportation hubs, ports, and airfields – the latter home to Chinese- and Soviet-supplied combat aircraft – off limits to the US air forces.

Early on, Navy and Air Force leaders tried various ways to apportion bombing responsibilities in the theoretically joint operation but none proved workable. Operationally, the services were guided by unique doctrines, methods of operation, tactics, and cultures. CINCPAC Admiral Sharp, as the commander of all US forces in the Pacific theater and the czar of *Rolling Thunder*, eventually established a system that was followed for the rest of the war. He created "route packages" dictated by geography and operational necessity. The Air Force was made responsible for air operations in Route Packages 5 and 6A, regions of North Vietnam closest to the air bases in Thailand. CINCPAC established Route Package 1, the area immediately to the north of the Demilitarized Zone (DMZ) and the closest part of North Vietnam to US forces in South Vietnam, as the bombing preserve of General Westmoreland's MACV. Finally, Admiral Sharp assigned Route Packages 2, 3, 4, and 6B, those regions abutting the Gulf of Tonkin, to the Seventh Fleet.

Few leaders of the armed services were satisfied with the command-and-control architecture of the Vietnam War. The Air Force complained, given its doctrine of centralized control of air power, that all US air forces in Southeast Asia should be led by one of its own officers. The Marine Corps, Army, and Navy had argued since the dawn of the 20th century that their special requirements for air support ruled out centralized control by a chosen service. Admiral Sharp affirmed that since the United States faced potential conflicts in the Pacific with the Soviet Union, China, and North Korea, two of these countries armed with nuclear weapons at the time, he had to be able to quickly focus all US air forces in the region on any emergent threat. He also argued, as had Admiral Chester W. Nimitz in World War II, that the vast Pacific was a predominantly maritime domain demanding an officer in charge with the professional expertise and background

to oversee it. Despite their doctrinal differences, the US military services at the operational level generally found ways to work together and to accomplish the mission. For instance, the Seventh Fleet's "Red Crown" cruisers equipped with advanced radar and communications gear, frequently warned Air Force units of approaching MiGs, and Air Force "Jolly Green Giant" helicopters worked with Navy search and rescue teams to save naval aviators who bailed out of stricken aircraft over the sea.

The real command and control problem of the Vietnam War, especially during *Rolling Thunder*, was the disastrous involvement of Lyndon Johnson, Robert McNamara, and defense department policymakers in the strategic and operational conduct of the war. Their general distrust and dismissal of advice from the JCS and the military in general dated from the administration of John F. Kennedy, the Bay of Pigs fiasco, and the Cuban Missile Crisis. Johnson and McNamara had given up on *Rolling Thunder* even as early as March 1965 and thereafter they focused US military power on preventing the loss of South Vietnam with US ground troops. As a result, Washington routinely dealt directly with General Westmoreland on strategic and operational matters, bypassing Sharp and "his" air campaign. Further complicating air operations was the involvement of the US ambassadors to Laos and South Vietnam, who often dismissed the professional advice of their military counterparts.

April 3, 1965 marked the first time that North Vietnamese MiG-17 "Fresco" fighters attacked a flight of Seventh Fleet aircraft. The next day, a quartet of MiG-17s shot down two Air Force F-105D Thunderchiefs operating near Thanh Hoa, killing the pilots. This aerial victory surprised American air commanders, who had considered the North Vietnamese pilots novices and their Korean War-era planes sub-par. North Vietnam's first fighter unit, the 921st Red Star Fighter Regiment, had only been established the previous year. The US Navy discovered the hard way that the preparation for air-to-air combat against Soviet foes in the Cold War had ill-prepared its first-line fighter, the F-4 Phantom, for the Vietnam War. Aircraft designers had emphasized high performance and the ability to carry out diverse tasks rather than maneuverability. The Navy's plane was armed with AIM-9 Sidewinders and AIM-7 Sparrows but no guns. Because Washington demanded that fast-approaching aircraft be visually identified as enemy fighters, guns and aerial dogfights became the order of the day.

The Johnson administration's fear of stoking greater Chinese intervention had a direct impact on the battlefield. On April 9, 1965, Chinese MiGs tangled with four Seventh Fleet F-4 Phantoms near China's Hainan Island. Naval aviator Lieutenant (jg) Terrence Murphy and his radar intercept officer, Ensign Ronald Fegan, shot down one attacker but the Chinese fighters downed all four of the American planes. There were no survivors. The Navy was not permitted to credit Murphy and Fegan's MiG kill for fear of highlighting China's hostile attitude toward the American military presence in the Gulf of Tonkin. Later in the war, Chinese fighters shot down five Navy and two Air Force combat aircraft. The only American aviator to survive those encounters was Lieutenant Robert Flynn of Attack Squadron 196 (VA-196) who was captured and only freed from prison after the war. On one occasion, the Pacific Fleet commander, Admiral John Hyland, pleaded with Admiral Sharp to launch an operation to rescue an aviator shot down on Hainan. CINCPAC refused, since the likelihood of success was slim and it risked war with China. But Sharp also knew that Washington would never approve such an operation and he was already at odds with his civilian superiors over operational matters.

The Navy's pre-war focus on fighting the Soviets also adversely affected air strike tactics. Naval aviators had practiced approaching targets at low level and then pulling up sharply to loft their nuclear weapons at the enemy. But Seventh Fleet aviators discovered that North Vietnamese air defenses were especially lethal at those lower altitudes. On the first two days of June 1965, enemy defenses shot down five Task Force 77 aircraft, killing six men and capturing two more. It also resulted in the loss of two RF-8 reconnaissance planes, two A-4 Skyhawks, and an EA-1F Skyraider. Fleet aviators learned that despite the danger from enemy MiGs and surface-to-air missiles at higher altitudes there was greater danger close to the ground. North Vietnamese antiaircraft artillery, automatic weapons, and on occasion a peasant's AK-47 rifle could take down a high-performance jet. Those weapons accounted for three times the number of naval aircraft lost to MiGs and SAMs during the war.

1968 Creighton W. Abrams, dominated the decision-making with regard to air, naval, and ground operations in and around South Vietnam, and Washington gave them great latitude in the conduct of combat operations. Westmoreland, and to a lesser extent Abrams, frequently pushed to get operational control of Seventh Fleet carriers, bombardment ships, and the Navy–Marine Corps ARG/SLF engaged in the fight for South Vietnam. Interservice cooperative agreements and the establishment in 1966 of Commander Naval Forces, Vietnam (COMNAVFORV) under COMUSMACV alleviated some but not all of the issues.

INTELLIGENCE

Throughout the war, the Seventh Fleet benefitted from the intelligence captured not only by its organic resources but by a host of higher-level military and national-level commands and agencies. The Office of Naval Intelligence (ONI) and the intelligence staffs of the Pacific Command and Pacific Fleet proved indispensable to fleet operations. These supporting organizations apprised Seventh Fleet commanders of international and foreign policy developments that might impact their combat operations, the extent of Soviet and Chinese military assistance to North Vietnam, the movement of enemy troops and supplies down the Ho Chi Minh Trail, seaborne infiltration of South Vietnam, and imminent threats to their ships and sailors. As one example of the latter, national and naval intelligence alerted Captain John J. Herrick, the officer in tactical command of destroyer *Maddox* (DD-731) in August 1964, that North Vietnamese torpedo boats were headed his way with intent to sink his ship.

The national intelligence establishment registered successes and failures, for instance presenting a clear picture to Seventh Fleet commanders of North Vietnam's military buildup prior to the Easter Offensive of 1972 but failing to alert national leaders that Hanoi was supplying its forces in the Mekong Delta through the Cambodian port of Sihanoukville. Moreover, postwar analyses revealed that some of the other side's intelligence and counterintelligence efforts at times compromised or negated US operations. The NSA and the Naval Security Group (NSG), with intelligence-collection sites in the combat theater, gathered critical communications and electronic intelligence. The Central Intelligence Agency (CIA) provided the fleet with imagery from satellites and U-2 and A-12 aircraft of enemy movements and concentrations. The Washington-based National Photographic Interpretation Center armed the fleet with comprehensive information on Hanoi's ground, air, and naval forces and their deployments.

Seventh Fleet ships also collected intelligence to support future US military and naval operations. Anticipating likely amphibious and coastal operations on the coast of South Vietnam, in 1962 and 1963, high-speed transports *Cook* (APD-130) and *Weiss* (APD-135) completed beach surveys and investigated potential landing sites from the DMZ to the Mekong Delta. With war on the horizon, in 1964 the Seventh Fleet upgraded its photographic intelligence center at Naval Air Station (NAS) Cubi Point, in the Philippines. That facility and Heavy Photographic Squadron 61 (VAP-61) based there kept two photo interpretation teams on standby for emergency Seventh Fleet calls for assistance. The Navy developed an even more robust photo interpretation center with establishment there of the Fleet Intelligence Center Pacific Facility (FICPACFAC). Throughout the war, FICPACFAC provided the fleet with imagery-based studies of enemy ground, air, and naval forces in North and South Vietnam.

Enemy Seaborne Infiltration

Before the major buildup of forces in Southeast Asia, most US naval leaders concerned with the security situation in South Vietnam doubted that North Vietnam was supplying arms and ammunition by sea to Communist Viet Cong insurgents. With pressure from Washington, however, then CINCPAC Admiral Harry D. Felt, ordered one-time patrols by Seventh Fleet ships to prove or disprove the existence of such an operation. Between December 1961 and August 1962, Seventh Fleet destroyer escorts and patrol aircraft, along with surface ships of the South's Vietnam Navy, searched the waters east of the DMZ out to the Paracel Islands and along the coast of South Vietnam in the Gulf of Thailand. The naval forces failed to detect evidence of a seaborne infiltration effort. The following year, however, Hanoi did kick off a major maritime program to supply Communist forces in South Vietnam. On eight occasions in 1963, 50-ton to 100-ton steel-hulled trawlers of North Vietnam's 125th Sea Transportation Unit delivered munitions to Viet Cong forces in the Mekong Delta. Adding to doubt about seaborne infiltration, an investigating group dispatched in 1964 to South Vietnam and headed by Navy Captain Phil H. Bucklew concluded that the Ho Chi Minh Trail and not the sea was the major conduit for enemy troops and war materiel coming into the delta.

A dramatic occurrence on February 16, 1965 signaled Seventh Fleet leaders that they would soon have a new mission in the war. The crew of a US Army helicopter flying along the central coast spotted a camouflaged ship on the beach in isolated Vung Ro Bay. A major battle between Viet Cong guerrillas and South Vietnamese military forces ensued. The allies found on the ship and ashore in the jungle 100 tons of weapons and ammunition, most of recent Chinese or Soviet origin. The Seventh Fleet commander, Vice Admiral Paul P. "Brick" Blackburn Jr, observed to the chain of command that the "event at Vung Ro Bay … is considered to be positive proof that sea infiltration is occurring and raises the strong possibility that at least a portion of the unconfirmed reports of the past were, in fact, true. Sea infiltration into RVN is now proved."

Admiral Moorer, then the Pacific Fleet commander, endorsed a proposal by General Westmoreland to stand up a major US and South Vietnamese anti-infiltration patrol. On March 9, 1965, Westmoreland boarded *Ranger* (CVA-61), the flagship of Commander Task Force 77, Rear Admiral Henry L. Miller, to reinforce the general's call for a coastal patrol. Two days later, Vice Admiral Blackburn established the Vietnam Patrol Force (Task Force 71) to execute the coastal patrol mission. By July 1965, Westmoreland and naval leaders agreed that the coastal patrol, especially since it was being conducted jointly with the Vietnam Navy, should be the responsibility of his command.

Accordingly, that month the Seventh Fleet turned over operational control of the coastal patrol effort to MACV and Rear Admiral Norvell G. Ward, then Westmoreland's Chief of the Naval Advisory Group. Ward established the Coastal Surveillance Force (Task Force 115) with organic naval forces to execute Operation *Market Time*. Throughout the war, however, Seventh Fleet P-3 Orion patrol planes, submarines, and other units teamed up with MACV's Task Force 115 to carry out the patrol. The US naval commands and Washington- and Pacific-based intelligence commands and staffs put together a first-rate analytical program that enabled *Market Time* to track the larger infiltrating vessels and determine their likely drop-off points in South Vietnam. Eventually, the P-3s carried equipment that identified the radio frequencies of infiltrating trawlers and monitored their communications. Superior intelligence collection and analysis, as well as the bravery and professionalism of American and Vietnamese sailors, led to the success of *Market Time*. But a negative factor

A North Vietnamese 100-ton trawler, first spotted by a Seventh Fleet SP-2H Neptune far out to sea, burns after interception in June 1966 off the Mekong Delta by US Coast Guard cutter *Point League* (WPB-82304). (NHHC)

was Hanoi's realization that it could keep Communist forces in South Vietnam, Laos, and Cambodia well-armed and supplied via the Ho Chi Minh Trail and the port of Sihanoukville in Cambodia.

Intelligence Collection in Laos

Following Diem's assassination by officers of his own armed forces in November 1963 and the accompanying disruption to the allied counterinsurgency effort, North Vietnamese leaders saw an opportunity to destroy their southern foe. In cooperation with their Laotian Communist allies, the Pathet Lao, Hanoi increased the flow of troops and supplies down the Ho Chi Minh Trail. Johnson and McNamara considered it essential that Washington acquire more precise intelligence on North Vietnamese and Pathet Lao military forces in Laos and the extent of infiltration on the trail. Accordingly, on May 18, 1964 Admiral Felt kicked off Operation *Yankee Team* that entailed aerial reconnaissance of select areas in Laos. Shortly afterward, Navy and Marine RF-8A Crusader and RA-3B Skywarrior reconnaissance planes and Air Force units conducted the first missions. The faster Crusaders carried out low-level sweeps while the larger and slower Skywarriors operated above 10,000 feet. Capturing electronic intelligence in Laos were Fleet Air Reconnaissance Squadron 1 (VQ-1) EA-3Bs based in Japan but operating from TF-77 ships and Danang in South Vietnam.

All did not go well. On June 6, a 37mm antiaircraft weapon downed the RF-8A flown by Lieutenant Charles F. Klusmann of *Kitty Hawk*'s Light Photographic Squadron 63 (VFP-63). He was the first of many naval aviators to fall into enemy hands during the long conflict in Southeast Asia. He escaped from a jungle prison camp and made it to freedom. Klusmann, and Lieutenant (jg) Dieter Dengler, who was shot down in Laos in February 1966, were the only Seventh Fleet aviators to escape from enemy captivity in the war. During

1964 and early 1965 carrier-based aircraft carried out 198 aerial photographic missions, half of the total completed in the joint Navy–Air Force *Yankee Team* program. These missions confirmed that Laos was becoming Hanoi's primary logistic pipeline to South Vietnam.

The Focus on North Vietnam

With the increasing likelihood during 1964 of war between the United States and the Democratic Republic of Vietnam (DRV), national and naval leaders decided that they needed a better understanding of North Vietnam's military and defensive capabilities. The primary mission of the Desoto Patrol was to gather all-source intelligence on North Vietnam's coastal defenses. In addition to sailors manning radar scopes and other intelligence-collecting gear, the Desoto Patrol ships boasted "vans" (windowless, box-like containers) emplaced amidship, inside of which operated Direct Support Units (DSUs) of

Lieutenant Charles F. Klusmann, the pilot of an RF-8A Crusader reconnaissance plane who survived a shootdown and capture in Laos during a *Yankee Team* operation, describes his ordeal to CINCPAC Admiral Sharp and Seventh Fleet commander Vice Admiral Roy L. Johnson. (NHHC)

the Naval Security Group. DSUs also operated from the larger Seventh Fleet warships. The highly trained intelligence specialists of these DSUs, normally communications technicians, monitored North Vietnamese manual Morse and voice transmissions and identified the sources of radar emissions. The DSU on board *Maddox* gathered information for use by the national security establishment, but another key responsibility was to alert the ship's officer in tactical command of any North Vietnamese military threats to the ship.

The teams conducting Operation *34A* had little success in their early 1964 operations, and a key factor was the lack of solid intelligence on North Vietnamese naval and coastal defenses. General Westmoreland wanted more detailed and accurate information, especially on the enemy's naval vessels that might hazard forthcoming *34A* missions. In response, Vice Admiral Johnson informed Captain Herrick that he wanted *Maddox* to gather all manner of intelligence on North Vietnamese coastal defenses, radar sites, navigational aids, and junk traffic. Shortly after *Maddox* entered the Gulf of Tonkin for the Desoto Patrol mission, Herrick learned from his DSU and from the NSG intercept stations in the Philippines and South Vietnam that the North Vietnamese were planning to attack his ship. Admiral Johnson characterized the cryptologic intelligence support of his command during the crisis as "absolutely invaluable." An authority on cryptology during the war later observed that the signals intelligence community "could be proud of its efforts that day" because "everyone in the Pacific command was aware of the approaching attack."

THE VIETNAM THEATER OF OPERATIONS

The intelligence stations in South Vietnam and the Philippines reported that on August 4 the North Vietnamese navy would once again attack the Desoto Patrol force. That night, far out in the Gulf of Tonkin, *Maddox* and *Turner Joy* reported being under attack by hostile vessels. Deciding that this supposed second attack required a strong US military response, Johnson and McNamara directed the Seventh Fleet to prepare for reprisal strikes against North Vietnam. Before that happened, however, Herrick informed his superiors that he had doubts about the events on the night of August 4. However, initial analysis by the NSA seemed to suggest that the North Vietnamese navy had carried out an attack. Persuaded, the president and the other top leaders of the national security establishment called for execution of the planned retaliatory strike. But the NSA's (and indeed the Navy's) combat analysis was flawed. Only a short time after the nighttime incident, agency analysts questioned the accuracy of their early assessment but did not inform the White House since they did not want to "piss off the president of the United States." It is now incontrovertible that North Vietnam's navy did not attack the Desoto Patrol ships on the night of August 4, 1964. Unaware of that fact, however, President Johnson directed the Seventh Fleet to carry out the August 5 strike, Operation *Pierce Arrow*.

Intelligence Preparation of the Fleet for War

North Vietnam's torpedo attack on *Maddox* and other hostilities in 1964 and early 1965 made it clear to American civilian and military leaders that US military forces would soon be engaged in full-scale warfare. The Seventh Fleet commander was determined to provide his air, surface, and submarine commands with a more comprehensive picture of North Vietnam's air and coastal defenses, regional weather characteristics, and other critical information. The Hawaii-based Fleet Intelligence Center Pacific (FICPAC) answered his call. In short order, the staff there produced new maps and charts, targeting aids, aircrew escape and evasion materials, and regularly updated enemy orders of battle. FICPAC also analyzed and disseminated to fleet commands aerial reconnaissance photographs. The Naval Weather Center on Guam provided timely data on the weather patterns in Indochina, northern and southern Vietnam, and the South China Sea that might impact Seventh Fleet operations. This intelligence support was not without problems. It often took days for aerial photographs and translated recordings of intercepted communications to reach the facility, be processed and interpreted, and then pushed forward to the combat commands. Often, valuable intelligence reached the combat commands too late to benefit the customers. The need to protect top secret and sensitive intelligence also limited who could see and use it.

The NSA also provided such information as the flight patterns of friendly and enemy aircraft over Indochina, surface-to-air missile sites, and bomb

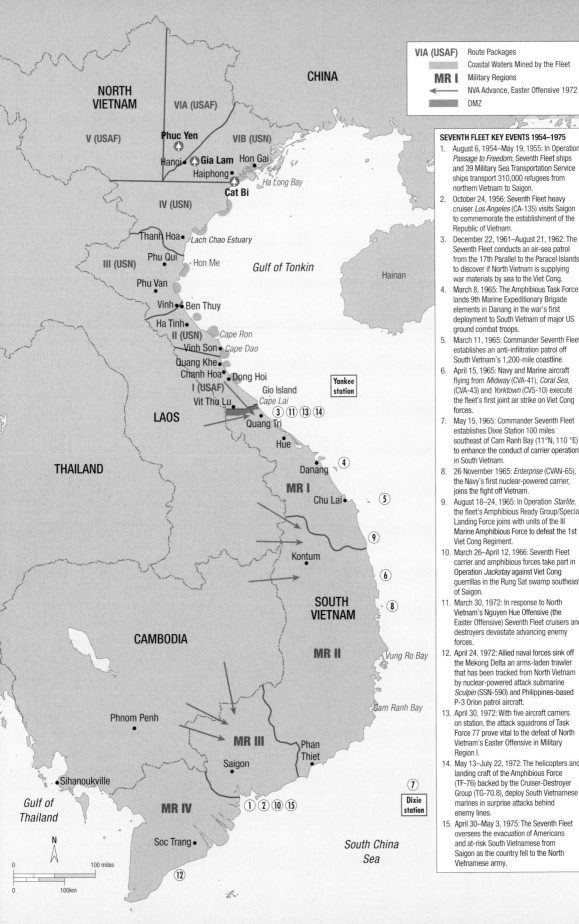

CHINA

NORTH
VIETNAM

V (USAF)

VIA (USAF)

VIB (USN)

Phuc Yen

Hanoi   Gia Lam   Hon Gai

Haiphong

Ha Long Bay

Cat Bi

IV (USN)

Thanh Hoa   Lach Chao Estuary

Phu Qui

III (USN)   Hon Me

Phu Van

Gulf of Tonkin

Hainan

Vinh   Ben Thuy

Ha Tinh

II (USN)   Cape Ron

Vinh Son   Cape Dao

Quang Khe

Chanh Hoa   Dong Hoi

I (USAF)

Vit Thu Lu

Gio Island
Cape Lai

Yankee
station

③ ⑪ ⑬ ⑭

LAOS

Quang Tri

Hue

④

Danang

MR I

Chu Lai

⑤

THAILAND

Kontum

⑨

⑥

SOUTH
VIETNAM

⑧

CAMBODIA

MR II

Vung Ro Bay

Cam Ranh Bay

Phnom Penh

MR III

Phan
Thiet

Saigon

Sihanoukville

⑦

Dixie
station

Gulf
of
Thailand

MR IV

① ② ⑩ ⑮

Soc Trang

South China
Sea

N

0   100 miles

0   100km

⑫

Legend

VIA (USAF)   Route Packages

Coastal Waters Mined by the Fleet

MR I   Military Regions

NVA Advance, Easter Offensive 1972

DMZ

SEVENTH FLEET KEY EVENTS 1954–1975

1. August 6, 1954–May 19, 1955: In Operation *Passage to Freedom*, Seventh Fleet ships and 39 Military Sea Transportation Service ships transport 310,000 refugees from northern Vietnam to Saigon.

2. October 24, 1956: Seventh Fleet heavy cruiser *Los Angeles* (CA-135) visits Saigon to commemorate the establishment of the Republic of Vietnam.

3. December 22, 1961–August 21, 1962: The Seventh Fleet conducts an air-sea patrol from the 17th Parallel to the Paracel Islands to discover if North Vietnam is supplying war materials by sea to the Viet Cong.

4. March 8, 1965: The Amphibious Task Force: lands 9th Marine Expeditionary Brigade elements in Danang in the war's first deployment to South Vietnam of major US ground combat troops.

5. March 11, 1965: Commander Seventh Fleet establishes an anti-infiltration patrol off South Vietnam's 1,200-mile coastline.

6. April 15, 1965: Navy and Marine aircraft flying from *Midway* (CVA-41), *Coral Sea*, (CVA-43) and *Yorktown* (CVS-10) execute the fleet's first joint air strike on Viet Cong forces.

7. May 15, 1965: Commander Seventh Fleet establishes Dixie Station 100 miles southeast of Cam Ranh Bay (11°N, 110 °E) to enhance the conduct of carrier operations in South Vietnam.

8. 26 November 1965: *Enterprise* (CVAN-65), the Navy's first nuclear-powered carrier, joins the fight off Vietnam.

9. August 18–24, 1965: In Operation *Starlite*, the fleet's Amphibious Ready Group/Special Landing Force joins with units of the III Marine Amphibious Force to defeat the 1st Viet Cong Regiment.

10. March 26–April 12, 1966: Seventh Fleet carrier and amphibious forces take part in Operation *Jackstay* against Viet Cong guerrillas in the Rung Sat swamp southeast of Saigon.

11. March 30, 1972: In response to North Vietnam's Nguyen Hue Offensive (the Easter Offensive) Seventh Fleet cruisers and destroyers devastate advancing enemy forces.

12. April 24, 1972: Allied naval forces sink off the Mekong Delta an arms-laden trawler that has been tracked from North Vietnam by nuclear-powered attack submarine *Sculpin* (SSN-590) and Philippines-based P-3 Orion patrol aircraft.

13. April 30, 1972: With five aircraft carriers on station, the attack squadrons of Task Force 77 prove vital to the defeat of North Vietnam's Easter Offensive in Military Region I.

14. May 13–July 22, 1972: The helicopters and landing craft of the Amphibious Force (TF-76) backed by the Cruiser-Destroyer Group (TG-70.8), deploy South Vietnamese marines in surprise attacks behind enemy lines.

15. April 30–May 3, 1975: The Seventh Fleet oversees the evacuation of Americans and at-risk South Vietnamese from Saigon as the country fell to the North Vietnamese army.

damage to North Vietnamese airfields. NSA cryptologists passed on to the fleet intercepted reports by the North Vietnamese on the local weather. NSA's "Songbird" reports, if they could be translated in a timely fashion, alerted search and rescue forces to the location of downed aircrews. The Seventh Fleet also benefitted from the information support it received from vessels reporting to NSA, signals intelligence ships *Oxford* (AGTR-1) and *Jamestown* (AGTR-3). Manning these ships, that alternated deployments to the South China Sea from 1965 to 1969, were more than 300 sailors and other personnel, some of whom gathered information from North Vietnamese communications systems.

Intelligence and Amphibious Operations

The lack of timely and accurate intelligence was a major factor in the Seventh Fleet's generally unproductive and sometimes casualty-prone amphibious operations in South Vietnam. The goal of Operation *Jackstay*, for instance, a combined and joint amphibious operation in March of 1966, was to secure the Long Tau River to Saigon through the Rung Sat swamp southeast of the capital. The Seventh Fleet contingent included a carrier, a cruiser, and amphibious ships and Marines. By the end of the resource-heavy, 12-day operation, few enemy troops or war materials had been found. The Viet Cong, alerted to the arrival of the allied juggernaut, had disappeared into the swamp. Allied leaders also partly blamed inadequate intelligence for the failure of Operation *Song Than-Deckhouse V* in the Mekong Delta's Kien Hoa Province in January 1967. Apparently alerted to allied plans, main force Viet Cong (VC) battalions identified in the area earlier simply hid out in the jungle. Villagers questioned by allied commanders reported that the VC knew the date and location of the amphibious operation weeks before its launch. Vice Admiral Johnson complained that "the excessive time involved in planning and coordinating" amphibious operations with MACV resulted in "completely stale intelligence." He observed that by the time of a landing the enemy had learned of it and "had flown the coop." Westmoreland also regretted that these operations rarely caught the enemy by surprise. *Jackstay* and *Song Than-Deckhouse V* proved to be the war's last major amphibious operations in the II, III, and IV corps areas. From 1967 to 1970, the ARG/SLF carried out a few other amphibious landings but mostly supported the Marine divisions fighting ashore along the DMZ in I Corps.

Specialized aircraft operating from the Task Force 77 carriers were the Seventh Fleet's eyes and ears during the *Rolling Thunder* and *Linebacker* campaigns. These units gathered intelligence that could in a very short time help the combat squadrons find their targets, avoid or destroy enemy air defenses, and determine the success or failure of their strikes. RF-8 Crusaders, RA-3B Skywarriors, and RA-5C Vigilantes photographed potential targets before strikes and photographed the results. These missions put the unarmed aerial reconnaissance aircraft and their crews at great risk from enemy antiaircraft artillery, surface-to-air missiles, and MiG interceptors. To capture the best imagery, the planes had to fly over target areas without jinking to left or right to avoid enemy fire. Despite their best efforts and the bravery and professionalism of the aircrews, these units lost a high number of aircraft and naval aircrews during the war. The North Vietnamese shot down 12 RA-5Cs and 20 RF-8s, killed seven RF-8 pilots, and captured another five men. Search and rescue units retrieved eight aerial reconnaissance crewmen from the sea or the jungle. During 1969 and early 1970, *Ranger* deployed unmanned Model 147SK Lightning Bug drones to gather photographic intelligence but the difficulty of operating in the maritime environment and technological deficiencies doomed the experiment. In the end, all of the fleet's Lightning Bug drones had been shot down by the enemy, fallen into the sea, or crashed on Chinese territory. The Air Force was more successful with its drone program, especially after encrypting related communications systems to foil enemy intercepts.

At the forefront of the tactical reconnaissance force were the RF-8A and eventually RF-8G Crusaders of VFP-63. The RF-8As of the "Fightin Photo" squadron carried stationary cameras with 3in, 6in, and 12in lenses. Upgraded RF-8Gs later introduced panoramic cameras that swept from horizon to horizon. Despite the precision of their equipment and the bravery and skill of the aircrews, however, unnecessarily restrictive rules of engagement sometimes negated the worth of the collected intelligence. As one example, early in the war strike aircraft could not take out a discovered SAM battery until the JCS staff in Washington authorized the mission. Moreover, the need to recover the reconnaissance aircraft on board a carrier, process and interpret the imagery held on their cameras, and launch a strike could take many hours and even on occasion days. Naturally, the North Vietnamese did not keep their SAM batteries in one place for too long.

The RA-3B Skywarriors of Heavy Photographic Squadron 61 (supported by the Atlantic Fleet's VAP-62) flew two-thirds of their missions over the Ho Chi Minh Trail at high altitudes and during the day. The unit flew the rest of their

AMPHIBIOUS ASSAULT ON THE VIET CONG (overleaf)

In this scene, destroyer *Orleck* (DD-886) is broadside to the beach and providing fire support with her 5-inch/38-caliber gun during a typical amphibious operation of the war. Similar actions enabled the Navy-Marine Corps team to engage enemy forces all along the 1,200-mile coast of the Republic of Vietnam. Here, landing craft deployed from Seventh Fleet amphibious ships head for the beach loaded with Marines, tanks, and recoilless rifles as Marine UH-34 Sea Horse helicopters operating from an amphibious assault ship ferry additional troops to a landing zone. *Orleck*, as well as light cruiser *Galveston* (CL-93), amphibious assault ship *Iwo Jima* (LPH-2), and landing ship dock *Cabildo* (LSD-16), took part in Operation *Starlite*, the war's first major amphibious assault. The August 1965 action 9 miles south of Chu Lai resulted in the destruction of the 1st Viet Cong Regiment. Learning from that disastrous experience, for the remainder of the conflict the enemy routinely avoided contact with the amphibious forces and relied on booby traps and snipers to exact a toll of Marines and sailors.

missions at night. The aircraft made low-level runs and used specialized infrared cameras to capture enemy movement. The RA-3Bs accomplished almost 1,000 combat missions each year. Squadron planes also photographed the coast of North Vietnam from the DMZ north to the 20th parallel to support Seventh Fleet's coastal bombardment operations. VAP-61 aircraft were especially skilled at identifying river crossings or "choke points" where enemy vehicles often bunched up to cross over. The carrier and surface forces were eager to pounce on these concentrations.

The most technologically advanced tactical reconnaissance plane of the war was the RA-5C Vigilante. Like the fleet's other reconnaissance planes, the Vigilantes flew along likely enemy logistics routes and carried out post-strike bomb damage assessments. The planes' KS-69 panoramic infrared cameras recorded black and white and color imagery. They also employed side-looking radars and a Passive Electronic Countermeasures (PECM) system to collect electronic emissions. The infrared cameras could differentiate between natural vegetation and other coverings used to camouflage enemy vehicles, way-stations, and underwater bridges. During one 54-day deployment off Vietnam in 1965, *Ranger*'s Vigilantes carried out 42 reconnaissance missions that collected 174,355 linear feet of photography. In April 1966 the cameras carried by an RA-5C of Reconnaissance Attack Squadron 13 (RVAH-13) revealed a camouflaged coal complex near Cam Pha on the border with China. Armed with this information, carrier planes destroyed the target. In 1968, infrared images revealed suspicious truck movements around a cathedral in Vinh. The next day, Vigilantes of RVAH-1 caught enemy troops moving surface-to-air missiles and launchers onto the grounds of the house of worship. Carrier Air Wing 9 aircraft wiped out the missile battery without damaging the building.

The Integrated Operational Intelligence Center (IOIC) was instrumental to the precise and timely exploitation of camera footage and electronic intelligence. A number of Seventh Fleet large-deck carriers operated IOICs during the war. IOICs could produce photographic prints and readouts of vast amounts of information in minutes. That support significantly enhanced the bombing effectiveness of Task Force 77's carrier planes. On one occasion in June 1967, the IOIC on board *Enterprise* discovered on photographs captured by RVAH-7 Vigilantes a surface-to-air missile battery so well hidden that previous missions had missed it. The carrier's combat squadrons destroyed the battery soon afterward.

Throughout the war, US naval intelligence worked to keep tabs on the North Vietnamese navy's small fleet of gunboats and motor torpedo boats. On a number of occasions, reconnaissance planes spotted enemy combat craft camouflaged in remote waterways or along the shore and called in strike aircraft to destroy them. Naval intelligence also supported warships conducting coastal bombardments. Reconnaissance aircraft identified North Vietnamese coastal artillery sites, some in caves, for subsequent destruction and warned allied ships of the danger.

A SPECIAL MISSION IN LAOS

Secretary of Defense McNamara, pessimistic about the effectiveness of the *Rolling Thunder* bombing campaign, put new emphasis on interdicting the Ho Chi Minh Trail. He concluded that a barrier of acoustic and seismic sensors emplaced at critical transportation junctures along the trail and the DMZ could hamper the enemy's flow of troops and supplies into South Vietnam. Since the Air Force lacked the right planes in the short term, the defense secretary turned to the Navy to fill the gap with its Lockheed SP-2E Neptune patrol planes. In response, the Navy established Observation Squadron 67 (VO-67) in February 1967. The naval service moved with speed to assemble, train, and equip the 300-man unit by McNamara's November 1967 deadline. The first modified SP-2Es, redesignated OP-2Es, deployed to the air base at Nakhon Phanom, Thailand, in November and mounted operations soon afterward.

Routinely, an OP-2E equipped with less-than-adequate World War II-era Norden bombsights, dropped one to three strings of seismic detection devices (ADSIDs) or acoustic listening devices (acoubuoys). The acoubuoys, originally designed to locate submarines, were normally released at 500 feet. The Neptunes dropped their ADSIDs at 2,500 feet and later at a safer 5,000 feet. Once embedded on the ground, the sensors sent relevant information to overhead aircraft and a processing center at Nakhon Phanom. The facility then used the information to coordinate air strikes against detected enemy vehicles and troops.

The nature of VO-67's mission put the nine-man crews and their planes in great danger. The aircraft often flew at low altitudes and in poor weather over the high mountains and thick jungles of Laos. Opposing their mission were hundreds of North Vietnamese antiaircraft guns of various calibers. On January 11, 1968, soon after its first missions, the squadron lost its executive officer, Commander Delbert A. Olson, and his eight crewmen when their plane flew into a cliff in heavy weather. On February 17 the enemy shot down another OP-2E, killing its entire crew, and during this period antiaircraft fire damaged another four planes. Shortly afterward, enemy fire shot up the Neptune piloted by Commander Paul Milius. He sacrificed his life so that his crewmen could bail out safely and survive. An Arleigh Burke-class destroyer later bore the name of the courageous officer.

On February 18, the Navy convened a conference to determine how to improve the survivability of crews and aircraft. As a result, it was recommended that the planes should make only single passes over an area brimming with enemy antiaircraft guns, fly at higher altitudes, and avoid operating in especially nasty weather. In July 1968, with the Air Force now deploying aircraft better suited to the intelligence-gathering mission, the Navy disestablished VO-67. Despite the fact that Observation Squadron 67 had suffered the loss of 20 crewmen killed and three OP-2E patrol planes destroyed, its emergency response to a high-level operational requirement earned it a Presidential Unit Citation. The sensors emplaced by VO-67 proved especially beneficial to allied attack squadrons hitting North Vietnamese troops moving down the trail and besieging the Marine outpost at Khe Sanh during the Tet Offensive of 1968.

Signals Intelligence

The Seventh Fleet's largest aviation unit, Fleet Air Reconnaissance Squadron 1 (VQ-1), targeted the electronic signals emanating from North Vietnamese air defense radars. Operating with the squadron's personnel were NSG communications technicians. The unit's initial complement of aircraft included 13 EA-3B Skywarriors and EC-121M Warning Stars. Later in the war, VQ-1 operated 30 EA-3Bs, EKA-3Bs, and E-1Bs. The unit focused its work on North Vietnam's Tonkin Delta, the Ho Chi Minh Trail, and the DMZ. VQ-1's most vital responsibility was to provide US naval units with near real-time warnings of threats posed by enemy SAMs, MiGs, and antiaircraft artillery. One squadron veteran remembered that he and his fellow EC-121 crewmen, electronic and communications intelligence specialists, frequently carried out 10- to 12-hour-long missions, seven days a week over the Gulf of Tonkin. Other crewmen included linguists capable of understanding the Russian, Chinese, and Vietnamese languages. When time was critical, aircraft personnel alerted naval commands in clear, unencrypted messages with information on the range, bearing, and time to enemy threats. During the Tet Offensive of 1968, five EC-121s and EA-3Bs operated daily over the Gulf of Tonkin. The enemy did not shoot down a single VQ-1 plane during the war, but the squadron suffered personnel and materiel casualties nonetheless. On July 15, 1967, for instance, a Viet Cong rocket attack wounded 44 VQ-1 personnel, damaged four EC-121s, and leveled squadron barracks and support buildings at Danang air base in South Vietnam.

The Enemy's Intelligence Effort

With regard to the success or failure of US intelligence-gathering, as the expression goes "the enemy gets a vote." The US intelligence community came to respect the professional skill, adaptability, and determination of their North Vietnamese counterparts. Fairly soon after the onset of *Rolling Thunder*, the enemy gained an appreciation of US rules of engagement and exploited that knowledge. Since US forces were prohibited from endangering foreign embassies, hospitals, houses of worship, and agricultural dikes, the North Vietnamese often emplaced surface-to-air missile batteries and antiaircraft guns around those sites. Knowing that the Americans would do all they could to rescue downed aviators, the enemy also set up clever ambushes to shoot down rescue aircraft.

The North Vietnamese developed a sophisticated understanding of US air attack patterns and methods. In that, they were aided by Soviet AGIs – small trawlers – positioned in the Gulf of Tonkin that alerted Hanoi when Alpha strikes launched

Gidrofon, a Soviet intelligence ship, or AGI, loiters off *Coral Sea*'s port side during operations in the Gulf of Tonkin. The AGIs routinely informed Hanoi when Task Force 77 carriers launched aircraft for bombing missions in North and South Vietnam and Laos. (NHHC)

from Task Force 77 carriers. The enemy also realized that when reconnaissance planes appeared over an area ashore, the fighter and attack squadrons would soon follow. They also knew that other reconnaissance planes would routinely visit a bombed site to assess the damage done. The North Vietnamese also became skillful at intercepting US communications, aided in part by some American commanders and aviation personnel failing to adhere to the protocols of communications security or because of poor encryption equipment.

Sihanoukville and the Failure of Intelligence

Chinese and other Communist-bloc freighters routinely offloaded cargoes of munitions at the port of Sihanoukville on the Gulf of Thailand. Cambodian trucking companies then transferred the war materiel, including AK-47 assault rifles, rocket-propelled grenade launchers, mortars, and ammunition, to Communist troops on the Cambodia–South Vietnam border. Since Cambodia was considered a neutral nation, the Johnson and Nixon administrations ruled out blockading the port, which international law would have considered an act of war. The US failure to stop the flow of weapons and ammunition through Sihanoukville vitiated the Seventh Fleet's overall anti-infiltration effort. For too long, US intelligence organizations in Washington disagreed with intelligence commands in the Pacific and in South Vietnam that the enemy was moving a significant amount of war materiel through Sihanoukville. The various commands dithered while the supplies continued to flow to the enemy. The overthrow of the government of Prince Norodom Sihanouk in March 1970 and the subsequent allied invasion of Cambodia finally confirmed the enemy's use of Sihanoukville as a major point of entry for arms destined for the Mekong Delta. Captured documents and cryptographic equipment revealed that between December 1966 and April 1969, ships delivered 21,690 tons of military supplies to the port.

With this supply line now closed to them, the North Vietnamese renewed the use of trawlers to supply Communist forces in the delta, but without much success. Of the 15 ships sent south between August 1969 and December 1970, 13 were discovered by *Market Time* forces and compelled to abort their missions. When trawlers discovered they were being tracked by the fleet's P-3 Orions or surface ships, they usually gave up the effort and returned home. In a new approach, naval units worked to track a trawler's passage sight unseen. The P-3s photographed the ship departing the Gulf of Tonkin and passed images to a submarine which then followed the ship through the waters of the South China Sea. Only when the trawler, thinking it had not been spotted, headed for the coast of South Vietnam did the trailing submarine alert US and South Vietnamese naval units to intercept the ship. In the latter months of 1971, *Market Time* forces destroyed three vessels, including a trawler with a carrying capacity of 400 tons. Chastened by this loss, the North Vietnamese did not dispatch another ship for six months.

LOGISTICS

Underway Replenishment

The Seventh Fleet's Logistic Support Force (Task Force 73), Service Squadron 3, provisioned the more than 100 Seventh Fleet ships deployed off Vietnam, up to 1,300 miles from the Subic Bay logistics complex and thousands of miles from naval bases in Japan and on the West Coast of the United States. The task force strengthened the fighting forces with fuel, ammunition, supplies, repair parts, and communications, towing, salvage, port service, and postal support and facilitated the much-desired sharing of movies between ships. The relatively small support force, operating on a three- to five-day cycle between Subic Bay, the Gulf of Tonkin, and the coast of South Vietnam, consisted of ten oilers, six ammunition ships, two stores issue ships, four refrigerated ships, and one combat stores ship. These ships averaged 22 underway replenishments every day, one-third of them at night and often in stormy seas. During the war, Task Force 73 delivered via underway replenishment more than 95 percent of the aviation fuel (41 million gallons in one three-month period) and ordnance (15,000 short tons each month) to naval forces off Vietnam. Fuel pumping rates for the newer support ships were almost three times more than their World War II predecessors. On occasion, ammunition ships delivered ordnance to cruisers and destroyers even as the warships bombarded targets ashore. In a given year, up to 97 percent of the fleet's needs for fuel, ammunition, and supplies was satisfied by at-sea transfer.

The introduction of new techniques and new classes of support ship markedly improved the logistical process. One such innovation entailed the use of assigned shipboard helicopters to deliver supplies to ships underway via "vertical replenishment." New, multifunction logistic ships such as fast combat support ship *Sacramento* (AOE-1) and the combat stores ship *Mars* (AFS-1) proved a

In an underway replenishment on October 1, 1965, aircraft carrier *Hancock* (CVA-19) takes on fuel from high-capacity, fast combat support ship *Sacramento* (AOE-1). Steaming alongside to receive similar support is guided missile destroyer *Robinson* (DDG-12). Two other ships await their turn behind the floating gas station. (NHHC)

boon to the logistic effort. The AOE, able to steam at 27-knot speeds, combined the functions of an oiler, an ammunition ship, and a cargo ship and was capable of supplying Task Force 77 with 165,000 barrels of aviation and ship fuel, ammunition, and supplies. The AFS, which boasted one of the fleet's first computers to process procurements, combined the functions of older stores and aviation supply ships. This floating depot, 581 feet long, could provide 118,000 cubic feet of refrigerated stores and 308,000 cubic feet of non-refrigerated provisions to the fleet. Communications relay ships *Annapolis* (AGMR-1) and *Arlington* (AGMR-2), deployed in the South China Sea, facilitated contact between the afloat forces and shore stations. *Annapolis* was the first ship to use a satellite in the transmission of a message relating to combat operations.

Salvage ship *Reclaimer* (ARS-42), fleet tug *Lipan* (ATF-85), and similar types pulled ships off rocks and shoals. Salvage ships freed from grounding *Frank Knox* (DDR-742), *Terrell County* (LST-1157), and captured North Vietnamese trawlers laden with munitions. Task Force 73's Harbor Clearance Unit 1 of medium and light lift craft raised vessels sunk by enemy mines in South Vietnam's inland waterways. Other vital specialized ships included hydrographic survey ships *Maury* (AGS-16), *Towhee* (AGS-28), and *Tanner* (AGS-15). The 1,000-bed hospital ships *Repose* (AH-16) and *Sanctuary* (AH-17) carried the latest diagnostic and treatment equipment. A staff of 24 doctors, 29 nurses, 250 corpsmen, dental surgeons, and other skilled and dedicated medical professionals saved many lives and eased the pain of wounded sailors and Marines. It generally took no more than half an hour for evacuation helicopters to fly casualties to a ship positioned off the coast.

A CH-46 Sea Knight helicopter lifts cargo from the stern of *Wichita* (AOR-1), a multipurpose replenishment ship, for delivery to another ship, as a second CH-46 stands by. *Wichita, Sacramento, Mars*, and other state-of-the-art logistic ships significantly improved the fleet's underway replenishment capability. (NHHC)

The upsurge in Seventh Fleet operations off Vietnam in 1964 put great strain on the existing logistic system. In the final months of the year, Task Force 73 delivered 1,300 short tons of supplies above the average issue. Early the next year, underway replenishments grew from 300 to 429 a month. It became clear to Seventh Fleet commander Vice Admiral Roy Johnson that he did not have the ships he needed to handle the increase in demand. Consequently, some of his fleet units did not receive fresh food. Other ships experienced shortages of petroleum, oil, and lubricants (POL), clothing, and other items. It took too long for logistic ships to make the 4,000-mile round-trip between the main supply depots in Japan and the South China Sea.

Shore Base Support of the Fleet

Backing up the Seventh Fleet's Task Force 73 was the Navy's vast complex of Pacific-wide shore bases, airfields, and other facilities. That logistic establishment, the responsibility of the Pacific Fleet's Commander Service Force, included the naval ship repair facilities and supply depots in Subic Bay in the Philippines and Yokosuka in Japan; the naval magazines in Subic Bay and on the island of Guam; and the naval ordnance facilities in Yokosuka and Sasebo, Japan. To strengthen and better coordinate support for the fleet off Vietnam, midway through the war the Pacific command assigned the California-based naval stations at San Francisco, Treasure Island, Terminal Island, Long Beach, and San Diego to the Service Force.

The problems experienced by shore facilities were similar to those that troubled the fleet's underway replenishment force. The depots in the Subic Bay–Sangley Point area, critical to sustainment of the fleet in the Gulf of Tonkin and along the coast of South Vietnam, were hard-pressed. During the first quarter of 1965, there was a four-fold increase in the number of ships steaming into Subic Bay for resupply and refueling. The naval magazine, which handled the Navy's priority ammunition needs, also had to provide 3,000 short tons of bombs and other munitions to the Air Force each month. The naval magazine was capable of storing 16,200 short tons of ammunition but, with the expectation of heavy combat in coming months, Admiral Moorer, then the Pacific Fleet commander, called for a storage capacity more than twice that amount. He was also concerned about shortages of ship and aircraft repair parts and materials such as up-to-date maps and charts. In the latter months of 1964, the supply depot in Subic Bay had to refer 75 percent of requisitions for spare parts to other supply facilities in the Western Pacific.

LOGISTIC SUPPORT OF THE FLEET

Underway replenishment, in which logistic support ships provided the carriers, cruisers, destroyers, and amphibious ships with essential fuel, ammunition, repair parts, and supplies (70 to 97 percent in a typical year), enabled the Seventh Fleet to operate almost continuously off Indochina from 1965 to 1975. The warships did not have to travel to distant support bases to restock. The oilers, ammunition, repair, and supply ships employed tried and true methods learned in World War II and Korea to carry out their mission to support the warships in the combat theater. An innovative approach that made its debut in Vietnam was "vertical replenishment" that involved CH-46 helicopters delivering cargo to the fantails of ships on station. The depiction shows the typical 3,300-mile, 21-day underway cycle in the South China Sea during which logistic ships delivered support to Seventh Fleet warships deployed in the Gulf of Tonkin and along the 1,200-mile coast of South Vietnam. Also critical to the fleet's combat mission were the naval shore bases, airfields, repair, ordnance, and supply centers in the Philippines, Japan, Guam, and on the US West Coast that provided the ships with comprehensive logistic support and enabled sailors to recuperate from their combat deployment.

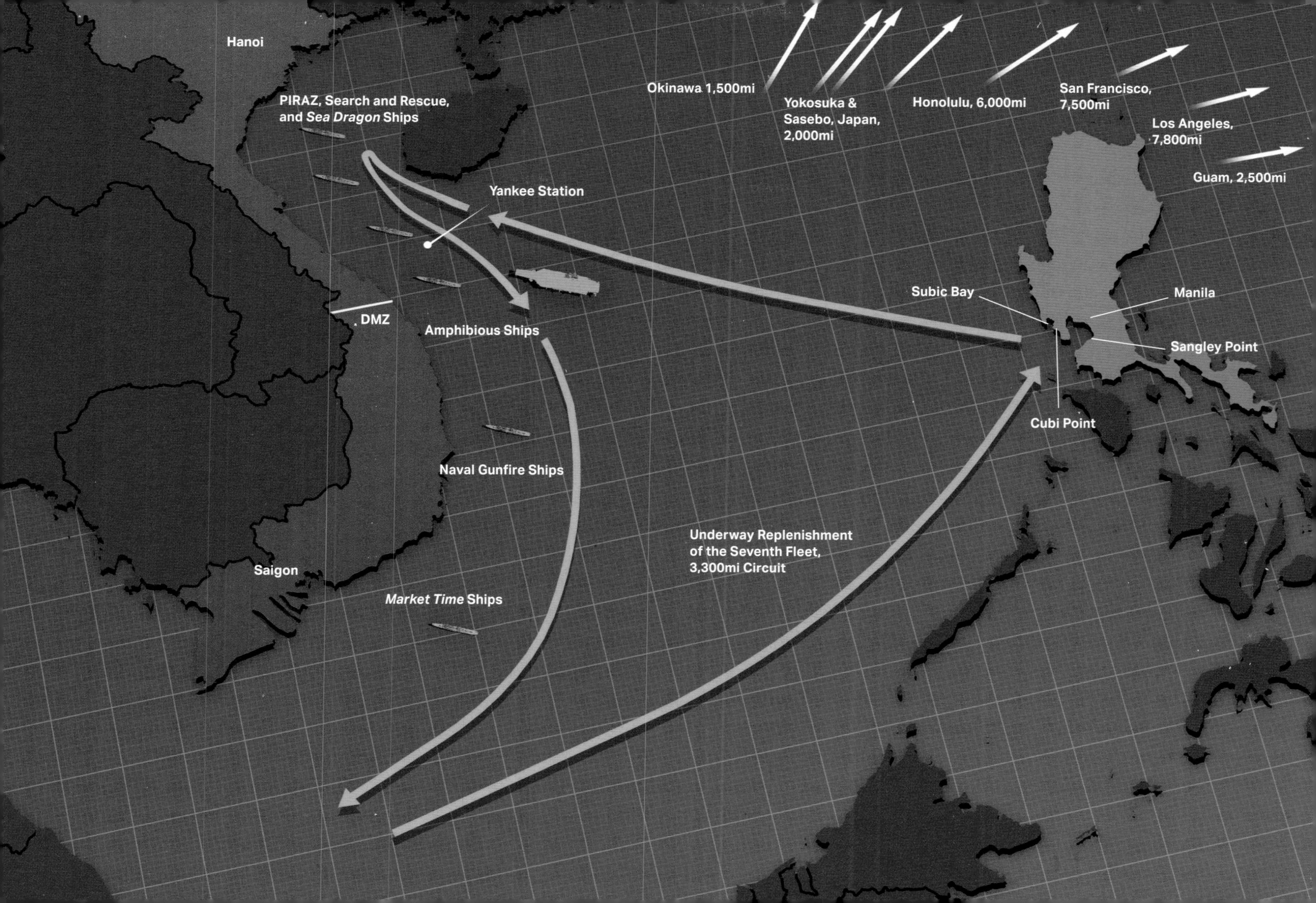

Hanoi

PIRAZ, Search and Rescue,
and *Sea Dragon* Ships

Saigon

DMZ

Market Time Ships

Naval Gunfire Ships

Amphibious Ships

Yankee Station

Okinawa 1,500mi

Yokosuka &
Sasebo, Japan,
2,000mi

Honolulu, 6,000mi

Underway Replenishment
of the Seventh Fleet,
3,300mi Circuit

San Francisco,
7,500mi

Los Angeles,
7,800mi

Subic Bay

Cubi Point

Guam, 2,500mi

Sangley Point

Manila

Moorer also worried that any slowdown of tanker traffic could have serious consequences for Seventh Fleet operations. At one point, the fuel facility at Subic had only a four-day supply. He called for the construction of a 265,000-barrel tank farm. The chain of command more than endorsed his request, providing for the construction of storage tanks in the Fiscal Year 1965 budget capable of holding 350,000 barrels of fuel. Going one step further, the Navy positioned two tankers in Subic Bay to serve as an emergency supply for the fleet off Vietnam. In general, the logistic shortages proved to be short-lived since the Navy devoted considerable resources to improving logistic readiness. These actions early had the service ready for war when major operations kicked off in the spring of 1965.

Throughout the war, the Navy continued to strengthen the capability of its key logistic facilities in the Philippines. By 1966, a $31 million construction effort in the Subic Bay area focused on providing additional petroleum storage facilities, an offshore fuel terminal, an enhanced electric power system, extensions of ship and ammunition piers, and new ammunition magazines, warehouses, and aircraft hangars. The Navy maintained a 60-mile fuel pipeline to Clark Air Force Base in northern Luzon. The Subic-Sangley area also

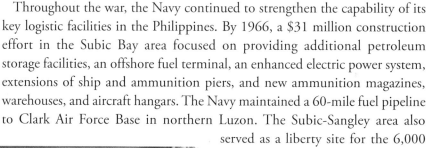

served as a liberty site for the 6,000 sailors and aircrewmen who arrived each month to enjoy a welcome if brief respite from the war. In 1967, as the Vietnam buildup continued, more than 15,000 Filipino and 500 American civilians serviced the 200 ships that pulled into port for resupply and repair each month, pumped 162 million gallons of fuel into the ships and aircraft squadrons, and executed a $20 million construction contract.

The logistic effort in 1968 at the height of the war was even greater with almost 17,000 Filipino and American civilian workers and 5,000 military personnel carrying out various tasks, including the provision in the first six months of the year of 600,000 rounds of ammunition to ships destined for the gun line off Vietnam. A fire that destroyed 18,000 supply items and a warehouse was little more than a momentary setback to the monumental logistic effort. The

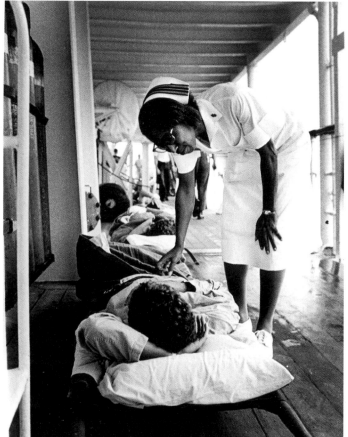

A Navy nurse tends to a wounded serviceman on board hospital ship *Repose* (AH-16), then operating just south of the DMZ. During the war, approximately 425 female nurses served in *Repose*, sister ship *Sanctuary* (AH-17), and the Saigon and Danang station hospitals. (NHHC)

support facilities processed almost 700 requests for supplies, pumped 43 million gallons of fuel and 4.4 million gallons of water, and handled 6 million pounds of mail. While the workload at Subic decreased during the last years of the war and the US withdrawal from Vietnam, it continued to serve as the primary supply point for the Seventh Fleet.

The naval air station at Sangley Point, 8 miles southwest of the capital of the Philippines on Manila Bay, underwent a similar buildup of logistic resources to handle Seventh Fleet aircraft based there. From the airfield, fixed-wing P-2V Neptunes and P-3 Orions and, for a time, Marlin P5M seaplanes, flew in support of the *Market Time* anti-infiltration patrol. In 1965, the command handled 24,000 supply items but by the end of 1968 that total had reached 61,000. In the latter year, Sangley Point managed the air supply to the fleet of almost 5 million pounds of cargo. The command also supplied and administered the naval air facility at Cam Ranh Bay on South Vietnam's central coast. During 1967 and 1968, the number of air operations at Sangley doubled from previous years and the command airlifted almost 3 million pounds of cargo to Cam Ranh. In 1971, the Navy closed Sangley Point and transferred resident squadrons to Cubi Point.

The logistic facilities at NAS Cubi Point were even more critical to support of the fleet's aviation forces. Established during the 1950s, by the onset of the Vietnam War Cubi Point boasted an 8,000ft runway, six berthing spaces for aircraft carriers and other warships, administrative buildings for the FICPACFAC, medical facilities, and barracks for sailors and marines. VAP-61, FAIR-1, and Fleet Tactical Support Squadron 50 (VRC-50) operated from

Civilian workers at Subic Bay's ship repair facility work on the 8in/55-cal. rifles from the forward turret of guided missile heavy cruiser *Canberra* (CAG-2). After months of heavy bombardment and naval gunfire support operations in Vietnam, retooling these weapons was a critical responsibility. (NHHC)

The naval base at Yokosuka, Japan, provided major logistic support services to the Fleet during the war. In port on the eve of the conflict are aircraft carrier *Bennington* (CVS-20), which would soon take part in Operation *Rolling Thunder*, an amphibious assault ship, and other combat and support vessels. (NHHC)

Cubi Point. A 55-building camp was established in 1966 to support the Seventh Fleet's SLF Marine ground and air units. Each month, Cubi provided the fleet with 3 million gallons of aviation gasoline and JP-5 jet fuel, handled 11,000 supply requisitions, and either repaired or shipped aircraft carrier equipment to the United States for overhaul. The air station also cared for the remains of 44 aircrewmen and ship's personnel killed in the fire that raged through carrier *Oriskany* (CVA-34) at Yankee Station in October 1966. By 1967, Cubi Point was the largest aircraft maintenance facility in the Pacific. The command oversaw 172,000 air operations and lifted 60 million pounds of cargo that year. During the next two years, Cubi lengthened its runway to 9,000 feet, incorporated the squadrons transferred from Sangley Point, and provided services to 65 aircraft carriers and other Seventh Fleet ships. By the early 1970s and the US withdrawal from South Vietnam, Cubi accomplished 176,000 air operations each year.

While 2,000 miles distant from the combat theater, the US logistic facilities in Japan, as they had during the Korean War, helped keep the Seventh Fleet's combatants well maintained and supplied throughout the war. The base at Yokosuka, 40 miles southwest of Tokyo and the fleet's homeport, provided ship repair, supply, administrative, communications, and medical support. The ship repair facility worked overtime to service the warships and support vessels arriving in port, 800 in 1967 alone. First-rate medical facilities and skilled staff members treated thousands of service personnel wounded in Vietnam who needed advanced care. Political protests erupted around Sasebo on the island of Kyushu and Yokosuka during the war over the arrival in Japan of nuclear-powered warships *Queenfish* (SSN-651) and *Enterprise*. That activity, however, did not slow the pace of work at Yokosuka or Sasebo. Moreover, by the last years of the war, it had become routine for nuclear-powered ships to put in at Japanese ports with little opposition from the population. The withdrawal of US forces from South Vietnam from 1969 to 1973 was reflected in the fewer number of ships putting in at Yokosuka and Sasebo and the lessened workload at their naval facilities. The value of both bases to the Seventh Fleet's strategic posture in the Western Pacific, however, as demonstrated during the war, prompted the Navy after the war to base the *Midway* (CVA-41) and follow-on carrier task groups at Yokosuka.

COMBAT AND AFTERMATH

THE SEVENTH FLEET AT WAR

In March 1965, after the Johnson administration's military pressure program had failed to curtail Hanoi's aggressive behavior in Indochina, the president launched the *Rolling Thunder* campaign against North Vietnam. That effort would be the Seventh Fleet's primary focus for the next three and a half years of the Vietnam War. The Navy's major combat elements unleashed devasting air and naval power against North Vietnam, eventually destroying much of the country's transportation and industrial infrastructure. Navy and Air Force squadrons made the enemy pay a high price to funnel troops and supplies down the Ho Chi Minh Trail. Nonetheless, the *Rolling Thunder* campaign and parallel operations in Laos failed to accomplish the mission of deterring Hanoi from fueling the insurgency in South Vietnam or destroying the will of the North Vietnamese people and the military capability of the DRV. Nonetheless, the Seventh Fleet used the experience to develop into a battle-hardened, first-rate fighting force that in 1972 helped defeat the enemy's Easter Offensive, severely degrade North Vietnam's war-making capacity, and convince Hanoi to end America's direct involvement in the long conflict.

The Seventh Fleet's participation in the Navy–Air Force bombing effort kicked off on March 15, 1965, weeks after it was scheduled to start. As would be the case throughout the campaign, heavy weather over North Vietnam had been a major factor in the delay. During the November to March northeast monsoon period, massive clouds, thick fog, and rain made flying especially difficult and indeed dangerous. The May to September southwest monsoon visited the same problems on air forces trying to operate in the skies over Laos and South Vietnam. On the Ides of March, 94 aircraft from *Ranger* and *Hancock*, components of Rear Admiral Miller's Attack Carrier Striking Force (Task Force 77), hit ammunition storage dumps at Phu Qui in southern North Vietnam. Dodging heavy antiaircraft fire, the attacking force, in the fleet's first use of jellied gasoline, or napalm, destroyed or severely damaged 21 structures at the site. This operation was the fleet's first Alpha strike of *Rolling Thunder*.

Seventh Fleet and Air Force combat squadrons continued the bombing operations they had conducted in Laos since 1964, providing air support to anti-Communist Hmong tribesmen in central Laos and attacking North Vietnamese trucks, refueling stations, bridges, and antiaircraft batteries on the Ho Chi Minh Trail. Many of the planes also flew "armed route reconnaissance" over the rudimentary roads of southern Laos in search of targets. A major effort was also initiated to cut off the enemy's logistical flow at key "choke points," mountain passes on the border between North Vietnam and Laos. The air attacks compelled the North Vietnamese to restrict much of their logistical traffic to nighttime, and took a heavy toll of trucks and infiltrating soldiers.

Carrier Operations at Dixie Station

Even as the Task Force 77 ships executed *Rolling Thunder* bombing operations in North Vietnam, other Seventh Fleet carriers provided air support to American and South Vietnamese ground forces in South Vietnam. On April 15, 1965, Navy attack squadrons flying from *Midway* and *Coral Sea* and Marine F-8E Crusaders operating from *Yorktown* (CVS-10) teamed up with US Army, US Air Force, and Vietnam Air Force (VNAF) units to strike Viet Cong guerrillas near Tay Ninh on the Cambodian border. General Westmoreland was impressed with the results of the operation and recognized that the Navy's carrier armada could significantly strengthen his air power resources. He was also concerned that there were not enough airfields in South Vietnam to accommodate more Air Force units. Another factor was the vulnerability of these airfields to enemy attack. On October 27, 1965, for example, Viet Cong sappers struck the Marine airfields at Danang and Chu Lai, destroying or severely damaging 40 aircraft parked there. In fact, the MACV command lost more than 3,000 fixed-wing and rotary-wing aircraft to ground attack during the war.

With these considerations in mind, Westmoreland asked Commander Seventh Fleet to establish a staging area off South Vietnam similar to Yankee Station in the Gulf of Tonkin. Eager to lend support, Vice Admiral Johnson ordered creation of a staging area 100 miles southeast of Cam Ranh Bay at 11°N and 110°E. Routinely, the Dixie Station carriers would conduct air operations in the less contested skies of South Vietnam before deploying to Yankee Station and the lethal environment over North Vietnam and Laos. By the end of 1965, the Seventh Fleet carriers had completed 26,000 attack, combat air patrol, reconnaissance, and CSAR sorties, one-third of all allied air operations in South Vietnam. The primary function of the Dixie Station carriers was to bomb enemy ammunition dumps and jungle redoubts, but also Viet Cong guerrillas assaulting allied infantry units. From June 10 to 14, for example, aircraft from *Oriskany*'s Carrier Air Wing 16 joined with other US and South Vietnamese units to beat back an enemy attack that had overrun the

COMBAT SEARCH AND RESCUE

Naval leaders recognized that rescuing those fighter, attack, and reconnaissance aircrewmen who went down in North Vietnam, Laos, or the Gulf of Tonkin was absolutely essential to the morale of those men but also to the thousands of Seventh Fleet sailors supporting their missions. The Navy and Air Force search and rescue forces took enormous risks – and suffered heavy casualties – to rescue men lost behind enemy lines and in the often-treacherous waters of the South China Sea. Navy surface ships, sometimes under fire from enemy shore batteries, were a vital component of the fleet's CSAR force. In July 1966, for instance, a helicopter from frigate *King* (DLG-10) retrieved one aviator from North Vietnam and four others from the sea. The following year, destroyer *Wiltsie* rescued nine aircrewmen. The ships also aided rescue efforts by refueling helicopters operating between the carriers and the rescue sites ashore or afloat. On September 20, 1965, the Navy carried out its first rescue of a pilot shot down in North Vietnam when a CSAR helicopter plucked an A-4E Skyhawk naval aviator, Lieutenant (jg) John R. Harris, from the ground 20 miles from Hanoi.

Despite heroic rescue attempts on numerous occasions, retrieving downed fliers who landed in the heavily populated route package areas assigned to the Navy proved to be a rare event. Many of the men who bailed out of their heavily damaged planes often hit the ground with serious injuries and then had to survive contact with enraged villagers. North Vietnamese air defense units also set ambushes for the helicopters and the fixed-wing A-1 Skyraiders and other support aircraft involved in a rescue operation. One tactic was to employ captured survival radios and parachutes to lure CSAR aircraft into an antiaircraft kill zone. Navy and Air Force CSAR units retrieved only a small number of men who went down in North Vietnam or Laos.

The North Vietnamese, with Soviet and Chinese support, developed an increasingly effective air defense force of MiGs, SAMs, and antiaircraft artillery that made it extremely difficult and costly to recover downed aircrews from North Vietnam. July 19, 1967 proved to be an especially hard day for the CSAR force. The enemy shot down or damaged five attack planes and CSAR helicopters, killing, wounding, or capturing six Seventh Fleet aircrewmen. But other CSAR efforts returned grateful aviators alive and well to their squadrons. For instance, on June 19, 1968, a UH-2 Seasprite helicopter piloted by Lieutenant (jg) Clyde E. Lassen sustained heavy ground fire and almost ran out of fuel before recovering two naval aviators from North Vietnam. The Navy recognized the crew for their courage and dedication to the mission and awarded Lassen the Medal of Honor for his leadership above and beyond the call of duty. During *Rolling Thunder*, the US CSAR units lost 27 men and 45 aircraft but carried out 276 rescues.

An SH-3A Sea King helicopter of Helicopter Antisubmarine Squadron 8 (HC-8) takes on fuel from destroyer *Carpenter* (DD-825) during October 1967. Fleet helicopters and surface ships worked closely and effectively in the search and rescue effort. (NHHC)

Special Forces camp at Dong Xoai northeast of Saigon. On other occasions, the Dixie Station carriers supported amphibious operations. In August 1966 Commander Seventh Fleet disestablished Dixie Station, since by then Air Force, Marine Corps, and Vietnam Air Force combat squadrons were well prepared to handle the great majority of air operations in the south. For the remainder of the war, however, Seventh Fleet carriers at Yankee Station continued to provide air support to the allied forces in South Vietnam.

Rolling Thunder

Despite the courage and bravado of many North Vietnamese pilots, the years of experience and advanced training of Seventh Fleet aircrewmen paid off in the war's early aerial battles. On June 17, 1965, for example, the crews of two F-4 Phantoms shot down two of the four MiGs that pounced on them 60 miles south of Hanoi. The attackers made the fatal mistake of banking away from the Americans who shot them down with air-to-air missiles. The training and professionalism of the Navy's aviators, even those who flew propeller-driven planes, enabled them to shoot down adversaries piloting jets. On June 20, 1965, four of *Midway*'s A-1 Skyraiders formed a tight circle close to the ground in defense against two MiG-17s and, when one of the enemy planes tried to break into the formation, the Americans knocked him from the sky with their 20mm guns.

Perhaps the most recognizable symbol of the air war over North Vietnam was the Soviet-made SA-2 Guideline (known to Moscow as the V-75 Dvina) surface-to-air missile. In the months following the Gulf of Tonkin incident, the Soviets provided Hanoi with missiles, launchers, radars, and command systems and sent in technical advisors to bring the North Vietnamese up to speed. The Vietnamese learned fast and SA-2s coordinated with antiaircraft guns and MiGs became a lethal air defense trio. On April 5, 1965, less than a month after the start of *Rolling Thunder*, one of *Coral Sea*'s RF-8A photoreconnaissance planes returned to the ship with pictures that positively identified a SAM battery being emplaced 15 miles southeast of Hanoi. The Task Force 77 commander immediately met with his Air Force counterpart and they called for strikes to take out the battery before it became operational. Washington shot down the proposal. Johnson and McNamara feared that killing Soviet advisors at the site risked even greater Soviet intervention. In July the missile battery became operational and, by the end of the year, 56 SAM batteries ringed the enemy's critical defenses around the country's capital and its major port. The Soviet advisors and their trainees, unlike the Americans, did not hesitate to employ the weapons against their common foe. The Communist allies fired an average of 15 SAMs against any US plane that appeared on their radar scopes. On July 19, a battery commanded by Soviet Lieutenant Colonel F. Ilinykh shot down an Air Force F-4C and on August 11 knocked down a *Midway* A-4 Skyhawk.

Midway (CVA-41), with a full complement of A-1 Skyraider, A-4 Skyhawk, F-4 Phantom, and support aircraft, steams in the Gulf of Tonkin. The other Midway-class ships, *Coral Sea* (CVA-43) and *Franklin D. Roosevelt* (CVA-42), took part in the *Rolling Thunder* campaign. (NHHC)

A number of Navy, Air Force, and Marine Danang-based aircraft focused on detecting, jamming, and disorienting SAM radars. The aircraft carried sophisticated electronic gear, commonly called "black boxes," to confuse enemy guidance systems and radars. The electronic countermeasure (ECM) crews used their equipment on the S-band (air search), C-band (height-finding), and X-band (fire control) radar frequencies used by the enemy. The planes also dropped chaff (strips of aluminum first used in World War II) to help blind enemy air defense systems. The most basic and effective approach taken by pilots to frustrate the pilotless weapons was to approach them head-on and at the last moment bank hard away from the threat. The high-speed SA-2 could not adjust in time to the plane's radical course. Naturally, this was not a tactic for the faint-hearted and it didn't always work.

Despite devoting resources to electronic warfare before the war, the Navy soon appreciated that much more was required to protect the naval aviation squadrons flying in the dangerous skies of Indochina. In Project *Shoehorn*, the Navy installed on its combat aircraft electronic gear that emitted a loud audio warning of an incoming SA-2. At the end of *Rolling Thunder*, however, Seventh Fleet leaders called for an even more concerted program to protect the aircrewmen and aircraft flying over North Vietnam and Laos.

The Air Force and Navy assault on the enemy's air defense command-and-control infrastructure registered initial success. On October 17, 1965, for example, a quartet of *Independence* A-4E Skyhawks, as part of Operation *Iron Hand*, destroyed a concentration of SA-2 SAM batteries at Kep airfield near

Hanoi. This work, however, was especially dangerous and it took a toll of brave and determined naval aviators. One of the most celebrated *Iron Hand* warriors was a *Ticonderoga* Attack Squadron 192 naval aviator, Lieutenant Commander Michael J. Estocin. On April 20, 1967, the intrepid pilot led a three-plane team that took out three SAM sites around Haiphong. Less than a week later, the North Vietnamese exploded an SA-2 near Estocin's plane, severely damaging it. Estocin tried but failed to keep his plane flying. The nation posthumously awarded the thoroughly professional and courageous pilot the Medal of Honor. The competition between the American and North Vietnamese electronic warriors went on for years, with each side responsible for successes and failures. The enemy worked to counteract US weapons and tactics. The North Vietnamese radar operators routinely turned on their radar for a short time to target a plane but just as quickly turned it off to confuse an incoming US missile's guidance system. The enemy on occasion penetrated US jamming systems to bring their SAMs into play and take down Navy planes.

By the end of 1965, the air war against the Communist foe was reaching a fever pitch. On December 2, aircraft from nuclear-power carrier *Enterprise*, captained by James L. Holloway III, a future Chief of Naval Operations, bombed enemy forces near Bien Hoa, the site of a major allied air base in South Vietnam. After deploying to Yankee Station, *Enterprise* joined *Kitty Hawk* and *Ticonderoga* in an Alpha strike on the power plant at Uong Bi near Haiphong. This operation marked *Rolling Thunder*'s first attack on a North Vietnamese industrial facility. Since the beginning of the campaign, naval aircraft had flown more than 61,000 sorties over North and South Vietnam. During that same period, the fleet's

Intrepid (CVS-11) deck hands work to position a pallet-load of munitions just transferred from a Task Force 73 ammunition ship to the carrier in October 1966. Despite the employment of new ships and equipment technologies, the ship-to-ship transfer of cargo still required the backbreaking and often dangerous toil of sailors. (USNI)

attack squadrons had dropped 64,000 bombs and fired 128,500 rockets in the effort to interdict the Ho Chi Minh Trail. When the Essex-class carrier *Bon Homme Richard* (CVA-31) completed a 1965 tour off Vietnam, the ship and air wing were awarded Navy Unit Commendations for their conduct of an unprecedented 12,328 combat missions.

President Johnson, who had already concluded that *Rolling Thunder* would not compel Hanoi to end its support of the southern insurgency, decided to try his hand at diplomacy. He eagerly accepted a Soviet offer to help broker a ceasefire, if only Johnson would halt the bombing. Despite opposition from Admiral Sharp and other US military leaders, the president put *Rolling Thunder* on hold from Christmas 1965 to the end of January 1966. Confident even then that North Vietnam could handle the worst of *Rolling Thunder*, Ho Chi Minh insultingly rejected peace offers, and during the interlude, the North Vietnamese reinforced the country's air defenses and pumped troops and supplies into southern North Vietnam and down the Ho Chi Minh Trail.

The air war entered an even more heated phase when combat operations resumed in February 1966. Increasing numbers of Soviet-designed, delta-winged MiG-21 Fishbed jets joined the fray over North Vietnam. The aircraft, relatively easy to fly and a fast climber, was capable of Mach 2 speeds. The fighter boasted two 30mm cannon and two Atoll heat-seeking air-to-air missiles. Later MiG-21s employed 37mm cannon, more Atoll missiles, and an improved radar. On April 26, 1966, several MiG-21s attacked an Air Force F-4C but came up short in the first instance in history of one supersonic plane shooting down another. The Phantom destroyed the attacker with a Sidewinder. That June, a Seventh Fleet F-8 Crusader made the plane type's first kill. Commander Harold Marr of *Hancock*'s VF-211 achieved a MiG-17 kill and a "probable" with a Sidewinder and his 20mm cannon.

In keeping with the concept of graduated escalation, during 1966 the *Rolling Thunder* attacks edged ever closer to Hanoi and Haiphong. Led by Commander David B. Miller, commanding officer of *Ticonderoga*'s VA-144, on April 13, 15 Skyhawks and Crusaders fought their way through heavy enemy air defenses to knock down five spans of a highway bridge between the port city and the border with China. That same month, Task Force 77 took a different approach to the bombing operation. An Alpha strike force, routinely mounted by a high number of fighter, attack, and specialized aircraft, was hard to miss on enemy radars. Instead, the fleet dispatched two A-6 Intruders led by Commander Ronald J. Hays that crossed the coastline at night and devastated the Uong Bi power plant near Haiphong. The pair then made it safely out to sea before enemy air defenses could even react. The Navy also adapted its carrier force to the needs of Vietnam air operations. Prior to deployment, *Intrepid* (CVS-11) offloaded the carrier's antisubmarine aircraft and embarked two A-1H Skyraider squadrons and two A-4 Skyhawk squadrons for operations in South Vietnam. When *Intrepid* deployed from Dixie Station to Yankee Station, the fleet added to the ship's air wing detachments of F-8 Crusaders and Marine A-4 Skyhawk "fighters" for protection against MiGs.

In addition to protecting the attack squadrons operating ashore, carrier aircraft defended the fleet deployed in the Gulf of Tonkin. The same three P-4 motor torpedo boats that had attacked destroyer *Maddox* on August 2, 1964 and lived to see another day, made a second attempt to sink Seventh Fleet warships on July 1, 1966. This time the attacking force did not escape. The P-4s emerged from a North Vietnamese port and headed for guided missile frigate *Coontz* (DLG-9) and destroyer *Rogers* (DD-876), 55 miles offshore. Aircraft from carriers *Hancock* and *Constellation* pounced and sank all three of them with bombs, rockets, and cannon fire, killing 13 officers and men. *Coontz* rescued 19 surviving North Vietnamese sailors who were later exchanged for American POWs captured in South Vietnam. A later North Vietnamese account related that as a result of the action, the men of the parent naval regiment "lost their faith in their ability to attack large enemy warships and became fearful of the enemy's superior ships and his technical and firepower superiority." That same month, other *Hancock* and *Constellation* aircraft sank or heavily damaged four North Vietnamese torpedo boats moored near the port of Hon Gai close to the border with China. Then in August, A-4 Skyhawks and A-6 Intruders sank four more vessels 50 miles northeast of Haiphong.

Seventh Fleet's POL Campaign

Admiral Sharp's subordinate commanders, working with the JCS staff in the Pentagon, put together a plan to target the POL storage sites around Haiphong and Hanoi. Deputy Secretary of Defense John McNaughton thought that attacks on the enemy's fuel supplies would have little positive impact on the war effort. Nonetheless, on April Fool's Day 1966, President Johnson and Defense Secretary McNamara, after the usual bureaucratic delay, reluctantly approved attacks on seven storage facilities. Determined not to spark further Chinese or Soviet intervention in the war, they mandated that the operations be conducted only on clear days and by the most experienced pilots who could visually verify targets. Washington feared sinking Soviet, Chinese, or other Communist-bloc ships in the port of Haiphong. This approach made it especially difficult for the attack squadrons to avoid the enemy's heaviest air defenses and it increased the likelihood of greater American casualties. Johnson later made the fuel farms at the Kep and Phuc Yen airfields, home to some Soviet and Chinese military advisors, off limits. Despite Johnson's authorization of the campaign, political developments in Saigon, hopes for a diplomatic breakthrough, and other factors continued to delay preparations.

Finally, on June 29, 1966 the POL campaign kicked off with a powerful blow by both the carriers and surface warships of the Seventh Fleet. An Alpha strike by 28 aircraft from *Ranger* slammed Haiphong's POL complex, devastating the storage tanks, with fire and smoke rising to 20,000 feet. That same day,

Constellation's air wing crippled the POL facilities on the Do Son Peninsula southeast of the port city. On the first day of July, other carrier formations hit the POL complexes at Dong Nham near Haiphong and at Bac Giang 30 miles north of Hanoi. In August, follow-on strikes against POL targets near Haiphong, which the enemy guessed were coming, faced one of the war's heaviest air defense concentrations. The cruisers and destroyers of Operation *Sea Dragon* complemented the air campaign, sinking hundreds of barges, junks, and other coastal craft, and apparently a Chinese merchant vessel, employed to transport POL. The heaviest action of the POL campaign occurred on August 25, when Navy, Air Force, and Marine aviation units executed 146 combat sorties. At one point in the campaign, the US air forces flew as many as 173 bombing missions in a single day and by September they had leveled most of North Vietnam's tank farms.

A tanker burns after attack by Task Force 77 aircraft during the unsuccessful US campaign to cripple North Vietnam's fuel storage and distribution system. Hanoi dispersed its fuel supplies throughout the countryside to thwart the US operation. (NHHC)

But the lengthy process to get White House and Defense Department approval for the campaign, and its overly restrictive rules of engagement that allowed the military forces little latitude in how they carried out their attacks, doomed the effort. Recognizing the intent of the campaign soon after its start, the North Vietnamese launched a massive effort to disperse fuel supplies in 55-gallon drums throughout the countryside. Soviet tankers started delivering POL to Haiphong in drums rather than by ship-to-shore piping. At one point, the Task Force 77 commander, Rear Admiral David C. Richardson, recognized the absurdity of his air crews attacking heavily defended and disbursed oil drums at remote locations outside of Hanoi and Haiphong. He concluded that the "risk-to-reward danger was cockeyed." His superiors agreed with him. Thereafter, the Task Force 77 attack squadrons focused their strikes on the enemy's transportation system. The POL campaign had hurt but by no means seriously degraded Hanoi's war-making capacity.

Rolling Thunder in Transition

The latter months of 1966 marked an intensified assault on the North Vietnamese transportation system and heavy air-to-air combat. On October 9, Commander Richard M. Bellinger, the commanding officer of VF-162 and a veteran of World War II and Korea, became the first Seventh Fleet naval aviator to shoot down a MiG-21 Fishbed. In another memorable operation, early in December combat squadrons from *Ticonderoga* and *Franklin D. Roosevelt* (CVA-42) teamed up with Air Force units in a 200-plane assault on the major truck depot south of Hanoi at Van Dien. Returning to the site two weeks later, the US air forces leveled most of the remaining structures there. By the end of 1966, Task Force 77 carrier aircraft had carried out 33,000 attack sorties in North Vietnam.

The enemy, however, exacted a price for American air operations in the skies over Indochina. Information released to the public on separate occasions by McNamara on the number of US aircraft lost up to that point in the war ranged from 854 to 2,083 fixed-wing and rotary-wing aircraft. The wide variance reflected the troubled management of the war effort in Washington. Similarly, when rumors of a shortage of aerial ordnance began to circulate, McNamara assured the press that there were plenty of bombs in the inventory. Not said was that many of the weapons, non-precision and less effective "iron bombs," dated from World War II and the Korean War.

In the early months of 1967, following another of President Johnson's fruitless bombing halts, for the first time the commander in chief authorized attacks on North Vietnamese industrial assets, including power stations, iron, steel, and cement plants, ship and rail repair facilities, and rail marshaling yards. He also allowed the fleet – after receiving specific White House approval – to hit select targets in Hanoi and Haiphong and along the border with China. As one example, *Bon Homme Richard* aircraft knocked out the electrical power plant in the heart of North Vietnam's capital. It was a bold and successful stroke even though the North Vietnamese got the facility up and running soon afterward. The new but still-limited operational latitude by Washington also enabled the US air forces to strike the key airfields at Kep and Hoa Lac. Johnson continued to rule out the mining of North Vietnam's ports, but on February 23 he okayed the aerial mining of the larger rivers in the country's southern panhandle, previously used by enemy coastal craft to escape the fleet's surface ships executing Operation *Sea Dragon*.

In the first operation, on February 26, seven A-6A Intruders from *Enterprise* established minefields in the entrances to the Song Ca and Song Giang. In succeeding months, Task Force 77 squadrons laid additional minefields with Mk-50 and Mk-52 magnetic sea mines and Mk-36 Destructors (magnetic/seismic mines based on 500lb bombs). Through the end of *Rolling Thunder*, Navy and Air Force units dropped 35,000 Destructors at river fords and bridge sites where the enemy's trucks had to concentrate in their journey toward the border with Laos and South Vietnam. The mining campaign registered initial success, but the ever-inventive North Vietnamese eventually found simple but effective ways to locate and disarm many of the mines. Naval aviators disliked minelaying operations because they still had to penetrate enemy air defenses to carry out the mission but could not enjoy the sight of a bomb exploding on target. Without sound, the mines simply hit a riverbank and sank soundlessly into the mud.

The intensity of *Sea Dragon* operations along North Vietnam's coastline increased significantly during this period of the war. Normally one cruiser or

As part of Operation *Sea Dragon*, a 5in gun of destroyer *Mansfield* (DD-728) opens fire on a North Vietnamese supply vessel hugging the coast just north of the DMZ in October 1966. On another occasion, the enemy fired back, inflicting casualties and sending the ship to the naval base at Yokosuka, Japan, for repairs.

destroyer focused fire on a target ashore while another ship, the "shotgun ship," suppressed nearby enemy coastal batteries. The enemy's coastal guns rarely hit the zigzagging and fast-moving ships but on occasion fire from their 120mm and 130mm guns struck home. On August 28, 1967, for instance, enemy fire demolished the forward gun mount of destroyer *DuPont* (DD-941), killed Fireman Frank L. Ballant, and wounded eight other crewmen. The following month, enemy coastal guns hit destroyer *Mansfield* (DD-728) off Dong Hoi causing five American casualties and taking the ship off line for repairs in Japan.

Rolling Thunder's Final Push

The period from March 1967 to March 1968 witnessed the heaviest and most deadly combat of the campaign against North Vietnam. After authorization by the White House, *Bon Homme Richard* and *Kitty Hawk* squadrons launched airstrikes against the enemy's MiG bases in the Tonkin Delta. Navy units hit Kep airfield, less than 40 miles northeast of Hanoi. On May 1, Task Force 77 fighters shot down two MiG-17s over the delta and shot up four more on the ground at Kep. Later, US carrier pilots destroyed or damaged another ten MiG fighters in a strike on Phuc Yen airfield. In fact, the Navy–Air Force focus on the Kep, Noi Bai, Kien An, and Hoa Lac airfields during the first months of 1967 not only resulted in the destruction of 20 North Vietnamese aircraft but put those bases out of action on numerous occasions.

The Seventh Fleet was now facing coordinated enemy air defenses of unprecedented lethality. At this point in the war, the North Vietnamese were operating 6,000 Soviet- and Chinese-supplied antiaircraft guns and missile launchers, most surrounding Hanoi and Haiphong, but in other key regions

CONFLAGRATION AT SEA

The enemy sank no Seventh Fleet warship during the Vietnam War, but operational mishaps devastated three aircraft carriers, destroyed scores of aircraft, and killed hundreds of naval aircrews and sailors. Ships loaded with tons of bombs, missiles, rockets, and flammable aviation fuel were potential powder kegs. The first major incident occurred in the Gulf of Tonkin on October 29, 1966, when a sailor improperly handled a flare that sparked a fire on *Oriskany*'s hangar deck. Extraordinary efforts by damage control teams saved the ship, but the blaze seriously damaged the carrier and killed 44 men. Of significance to the *Rolling Thunder* campaign, the fire took *Oriskany* off line for repairs until June 1967.

On July 29, 1967, an even greater calamity befell the Seventh Fleet. *Forrestal*, only days after arriving at Yankee Station and beginning combat operations, suffered a similar catastrophe. Faulty equipment set off a 5in Zuni rocket that punctured the fuel drop-tank of Lieutenant Commander Frederick White's A-4E Skyhawk. The blast killed him and engulfed his plane in a ball of flame. Lieutenant Commander, later Senator and presidential contender John S. McCain, and other aircrews had to leap from their planes to escape exploding ordnance. The fire spread rapidly, detonating bombs and igniting other fuel-filled aircraft. Ignoring the danger, flight deck crewmen rushed to contain the blaze and many paid with their lives as the conflagration spread across the flight deck and seeped into the hangar deck below. The fire killed 134 air wing and ship's personnel and seriously injured another 161 men. Damage to the ship and the aircraft on board was enormous. The blaze destroyed 21 planes and sent *Forrestal* back to the ship's homeport, Norfolk, Virginia, for $72 million in repairs and replacement of aircraft. The carrier eventually returned to service, but did not rejoin Task Force 77 off Vietnam.

A carrier fire also ravaged *Enterprise*, engaged in an exercise off Hawaii before being deployed to Yankee Station. On January 14, 1969, the accidental ignition of a Zuni rocket engulfed the flight deck in flame as bombs and fuel exploded. It took damage control teams three hours to bring the blaze under control. The fire killed 28 men, seriously injured 62, and destroyed 15 aircraft.

Repairs to the ship and aircraft replacements cost $56 million. *Enterprise* finally joined Task Force 77, but the fire had delayed the ship's contribution to the war effort for nine months.

The Navy learned many vital lessons from the carrier fires. Despite the heroism of many sailors, the incidents revealed problems with the Navy's fire-fighting procedures. For instance, when some teams on *Forrestal* fought the fire with foam, other teams used water that washed away the foam. The training film *Learn or Burn*, which employed actual flight deck film of the *Forrestal* tragedy, was viewed by sailors for many years afterward. Admiral Moorer, Chief of Naval Operations in 1967, tasked Rear Admiral Holloway, then in charge of the Navy staff's Strike Warfare Division, to find solutions to the carrier fire problem. Holloway's study called for cost-effective and practical measures to ensure the proper handling of fuel and explosives and to improve fire-fighting procedures. Moorer, especially pleased with the sensible recommendations, pushed their implementation throughout the fleet. The Navy experienced no other major carrier fires off Vietnam and indeed not for the rest of the century.

Firefighting teams turn their hoses on burning aircraft strewn across the flight deck of carrier *Forrestal*. The conflagration put the ship out of commission and *Forrestal* never returned to Yankee Station. Fires on board *Oriskany*, *Forrestal*, and *Enterprise* during the war took a heavy toll of naval aircrews, aircraft, and ships. (NHHC)

as well. Increasing numbers of MiG-17s, MiG-19s, and MiG-21s, some of them flown by North Korean pilots, battled Navy and Air Force fighters for control of the skies. Tens of thousands of Chinese and North Vietnamese construction troops, engineers, and civilians worked night and day to repair or replace rail lines, bridges, and key roadways. To lessen the pressure on the transportation system, in the fall Hanoi evacuated to rural districts all those civilians in the major cities who were not essential to the government, the military, or civil defense.

Navy chaplains offer prayers as *Oriskany* sailors pay their respects to their shipmates whose remains have arrived at the Subic Bay naval base following a catastrophic carrier fire. (NHHC)

Guideline surface-to-air missiles and antiaircraft guns claimed more and more naval aircrewmen and aircraft. In August 1967, the enemy launched 249 SAMs at US aircraft. On the 13th, two SA-2s brought down three Skyhawks when the enemy's electronic warriors neutralized the US jamming system. North Vietnamese missiles and antiaircraft guns downed 16 Seventh Fleet planes that month. In keeping with their concepts of leadership and professionalism, Task Force 77's wing and squadron commanders and executive officers more often than not personally led the combat strikes into North Vietnam. These dedicated naval aviators, however, paid a price for their courage and dedication to the mission. During the war, 67 Seventh Fleet wing and squadron commanders and squadron executive officers were killed in action as were 250 other aircrewmen.

From September to the end of the year, the air wings of five Task Force 77 carriers hit sites in Haiphong, Hon Gai, and Cam Pha, the latter two ports close to the border with China and previously considered off limits. The targets included docks, storage buildings, ship and boat yards, and harbor craft. In 1967, Task Force 77 executed an unprecedented 77,000 combat and support sorties. The combat squadrons severed or badly damaged 1,000 bridges and destroyed 700 trucks, 400 locomotives and rail cars, and 3,200 coastal and river craft. The electronic warfare offensive by the Air Force and the Navy was also on the verge of operational success as the majority of enemy SAMs fired during August went out of control or self-destructed. North Vietnamese commanders and political commissars had to redouble their efforts to keep up the morale of their air defense forces. Despite the prodigious US effort, it was not enough to alter the course of the war.

The *Rolling Thunder* air campaign and the operations to limit enemy use of the Ho Chi Minh Trail in Laos did not prevent North Vietnam from launching a massive military effort in South Vietnam. At the end of January 1968, troops of the People's Army of Vietnam (PAVN) and their Viet Cong allies attacked

American and South Vietnamese soldiers in Saigon, Hue, and 36 of the country's 44 provincial capitals. President Johnson was particularly concerned that the enemy would capture the combat outpost of Khe Sanh in northwest South Vietnam and overwhelm the US Marine regiment defending the base. He remembered how Ho Chi Minh's forces had surrounded and destroyed the cream of the French Army at Dien Bien Phu in 1954, which resulted in the withdrawal of France from its colonies in Indochina. Task Force 77 teamed up with the other US and South Vietnamese air forces to prevent that outcome at Khe Sanh. In Operation *Niagara*, during February and March Seventh Fleet carriers carried out 3,000 attack sorties and with Air Force B-52 and tactical air units, and Army helicopters, decimated the North Vietnamese attacking forces around the base. Despite the heavy weather of the northeast monsoon, which severely impacted flight operations, the fleet squadrons focused their attention on the supply routes into South Vietnam. The US, South Vietnamese, South Korean, and Australian ground forces soon recovered from the initial shock of the Tet Offensive to liberate all those population centers taken by the enemy and inflicted 100,000 casualties on the Communist attackers. Nonetheless, the Tet Offensive was a strategic victory for Hanoi. Many Americans, and especially President Johnson, now considered the war unwinnable, a huge drain on US human and materiel resources, and a source of great social upheaval in the United States. As a result, on March 31, 1968 the president addressed the American people, announcing a halt to US bombing operations north of the 19th parallel in North Vietnam, an offer to negotiate with Hanoi to end the war, and his decision not to seek a second term as president.

Rolling Thunder did not end when Johnson halted bombing north of the 19th parallel. Heavy fighting still raged in South Vietnam during the months after Tet. The Seventh Fleet's primary mission during this period was to interdict enemy supply lines north of the DMZ. Since US operations in this area far from North Vietnam's border with China posed little risk of stimulating Beijing to launch a major intervention, Washington gave operational commanders greater latitude to manage the effort. Vice Admiral William F. Bringle, Commander Seventh Fleet, focused the heavy combat power of Task Force 77 on three critical choke points in North Vietnam's southern panhandle – at Ha Tinh, Vinh, and Phu Dien Chau. River and other water obstacles at these points, as well as the

Battle commanders at work on the bridge of *Hancock*. From left to right are Vice Admiral William F. Bringle, Commander Seventh Fleet; John J. Hyland, Commander in Chief, Pacific Fleet; and Captain Howard E. Greer, the carrier's commanding officer. (NHHC)

narrowness of the coastal plain there, posed significant challenges to the enemy's logistical effort. In continuous, day-night operations, individual carrier task groups bombed and mined bridges, ferry crossing points, truck parks, and fuel and ammunition staging areas. Cruisers and destroyers of the *Sea Dragon* force bombarded many of the same sites and hunted the enemy's waterborne logistics craft trying to transport supplies southward.

While friendly fire incidents did not happen often during *Rolling Thunder*, June 1968 witnessed a number of incidents in which air-launched weapons inflicted personnel and materiel casualties on US and Australian warships operating in waters east and northeast of the DMZ. At night on the 16th rocket and automatic weapons fire sank US Navy Swift boat PCF-19, killing four American sailors and narrowly missing guided missile cruiser *Boston* (CAG-1) and Coast Guard cutter *Point Dume* (WPB-82325). The following night, air-launched missiles hit Australian destroyer *Hobart*, killing two sailors, wounding others, and damaging the ship. Bringle immediately launched an investigation that concluded that Air Force F-4 Phantoms had fired their weapons at what they thought were North Vietnamese helicopters. The Air Force and the Navy took quick action to prevent a repeat of these incidents.

In August, Admiral Bringle concentrated his fleet's combat power on Ha Tinh, the most critical link in the transportation network of southern North Vietnam. The US operations were so effective there that enemy truck traffic backed up behind the Song Ha Vang, becoming prey to air and naval gunfire attack. That month, aided by the rain and mud of the seasonal monsoon, Seventh Fleet units destroyed or shot up a record-breaking 600 trucks. In September, the *Sea Dragon* force put a crimp on the enemy's seaborne effort, sinking or damaging 1,000 coastal vessels. By October, the North Vietnamese units trying to transport supplies south had on hand a paltry 1,000 tons of materiel. These successes came with a cost in American lives and materiel, however. During *Rolling Thunder*, enemy coastal guns fired on 68 *Sea Dragon* ships, hitting 29 of them. Counterbattery fire forced 19 Seventh Fleet warships to withdraw from the gunline for repairs. On September 19 near Vinh, an F-8C Crusader piloted by Lieutenant Anthony J. Nargi destroyed a MiG-21. During *Rolling Thunder*, Navy combat aircraft shot down 32 MiGs, and the Air Force 81 MiGs, almost all with Sidewinder and Sparrow air-to-air missiles but a few with 20mm gunfire. The fleet's panhandle interdiction campaign from April to October 1968 – largely free from Washington's interference – was not a major turning point in the war, but it significantly hampered the enemy's ability to support the post-Tet battles in Military Region I (MR I).

On October 31, just before the national election of 1968, Johnson ended the Navy–Air Force *Rolling Thunder* campaign in all of North Vietnam. The Seventh Fleet had expended enormous effort and suffered heavy losses of men and machines to do its part in the war. Fleet operations carried out in the skies of North Vietnam and Laos and in the waters of the Gulf of Tonkin were made

COASTAL INTERDICTION, 1968

Seventh Fleet combat forces not only bombed enemy supply lines along the Ho Chi Minh Trail in Laos and Cambodia throughout the war, but also worked to interdict Hanoi's road, rail, and inland waterway transportation system in North Vietnam's southern panhandle. Following President Johnson's cessation of bombing north of the 19th parallel in March 1968, Seventh Fleet aircraft carriers mined the waters off the Vinh, Ha Tinh, and Phu Dien Chau "chokepoints" and bombed bridges, ferry crossings, and road traffic in the geographically constricted region between the 18th and 19th parallels. Simultaneously, warships of the Cruiser-Destroyer Group (Task Group 70.8), including Royal Australian Navy destroyer *Hobart* (D-39), concentrated their fire on enemy logistic targets ashore and against waterborne logistics craft (WBLCs) loaded with munitions and trying to make their way south. By October 31 and the end of Operation *Rolling Thunder*, this Seventh Fleet operation had reduced to a trickle the enemy's logistic flow through the panhandle and along the coast.

especially difficult by an untenable wartime strategy that enabled unhindered Communist-bloc support to Hanoi. Other culprits included unduly restrictive rules of engagement mandated by Washington and at times heavy monsoonal weather. The fleet did compel Hanoi to divert massive resources to the air and coastal defenses of North Vietnam. *Rolling Thunder* also increased the difficulty of combat operations for PAVN and Viet Cong forces in South Vietnam that were often short of troop reinforcements and supplies. And the almost four-year experience served to improve the fleet's combat capability. On balance, however, *Rolling Thunder* was a failure. It did not achieve its twin objectives of ending Hanoi's support for the southern insurgency or severing the enemy's line of communication between North and South Vietnam.

Targeting the Ho Chi Minh Trail

The primary major mission of the Navy and the Air Force after the October 1968 bombing halt in North Vietnam was to ramp up interdiction operations on the Ho Chi Minh Trail. By then, the North Vietnamese had developed a comprehensive and effective system for moving troop reinforcements and supplies into South Vietnam. Using conscripted Laotian laborers, North Vietnamese troops, and Chinese engineers, Hanoi built additional roads, bypasses, and underwater bridges which were often invisible under camouflage and jungle foliage. By 1968, the enemy was operating 10,000 trucks on the trail and each month as many as 4,500 troops and 300 tons of supplies passed through to South Vietnam.

Since the Johnson and Nixon administrations adhered to the Geneva Agreement of 1962 barring foreign troops from Laos, Washington employed technology to monitor Communist activities on the trail. The US air forces executed Igloo White, which entailed aircraft dropping and embedding seismic and acoustic sensors all along the trail. This equipment could pick up the sound or motion of trucks and soldiers working their way southward. The sensors

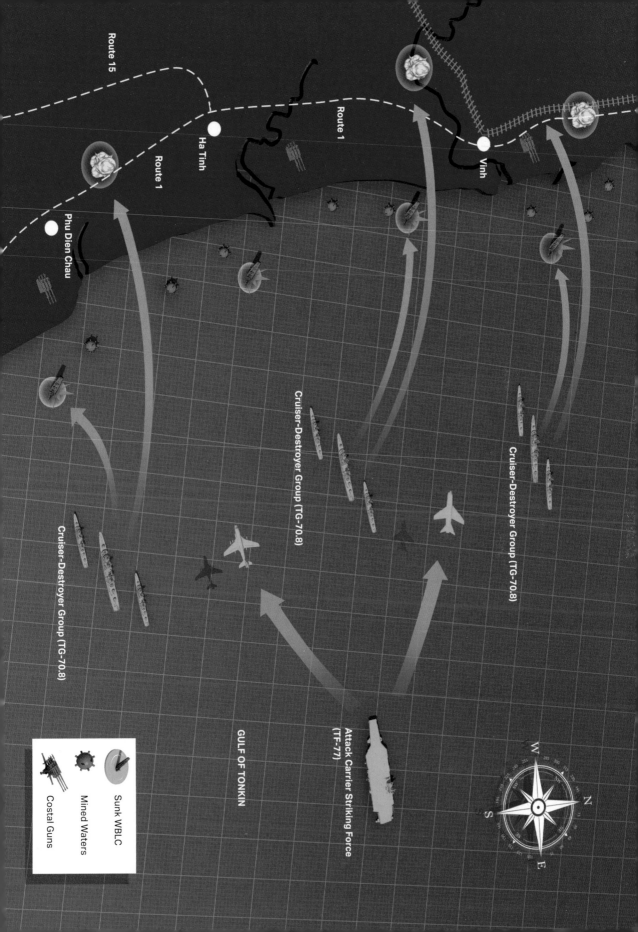

transmitted the information to aircraft overhead that in turn passed it on to an intelligence fusion center at the Nakon Phanom air base in Thailand. Attack aircraft were then vectored to the site to attack the vehicles and personnel. US aircraft dropped more than 20,000 sensors in Laos from 1968 to 1972. With the support of the sensor program, Navy and Air Force attack aircraft executed a series of seven strike operations named *Commando Hunt* that focused on destroying enemy trucks and cratering roads leading to and from the Mu Gia and Ban Karai mountain passes between North Vietnam and Laos.

Key to US air operations on the trail were the Navy's all-weather, day-night A-6 Intruder attack planes, as well as the Air Force's heavily armed AC-47, AC-119, and AC-130 gunships and B-52 bombers. Intruders proved to be especially suited to the trail interdiction campaign. The plane's airborne moving target indicator (AMTI), a radar, could pick up a truck at night moving more than 5mph. But as with many other operations in Southeast Asia, Washington's rules of engagement compromised tactical success. Before accompanying A-7 Corsairs, F-4 Phantoms, and A-4 Skyhawks could fire their weapons at a truck, an A-6 pilot had to verify the identity of the target by dropping a flare. That action, however, caused North Vietnamese truck drivers to screech to a halt, effectively blinding the AMTI. The Navy found the Air Force's Combat Skyspot, a ground-based radar, more effective at pinpointing targets for nighttime attack.

With only a few, special mission strikes being launched into North Vietnam from late 1968 to early 1972, Task Force 77 reduced the number of carriers routinely operating at Yankee Station to two or three. Several of the ships deployed there were older, materiel-casualty-prone ones, such as *Shangri-La* (CVS-38), commissioned in World War II and before Vietnam tasked with hunting Soviet submarines. The number of attack sorties executed outside of North Vietnam each month by fleet aircraft during the 1968–71 period dropped from the *Rolling Thunder* high of 6,000 to as few as 1,000. In this three-year period, the Seventh Fleet, in the process losing 130 aircraft and many of their crews, dropped over 700,000 tons of ordnance on the enemy in Laos and South Vietnam.

Carrier planes dropped 1,000lb Mk-40 and 500lb Mk-36 Destructor magnetic or seismic mines in addition to conventional ordnance. American military leaders gauged the success of these operations based on the number of trucks that aviators reported destroyed. The difficulty of determining whether a truck had been put out of action or merely banged up and the natural inclination to inflate successes, however, gave US leaders an inaccurate sense of accomplishment. A Seventh Air Force commander observed at one point that the air crews had credited the destruction of twice as many trucks as Hanoi had in its entire inventory! Moreover, the North Vietnamese and their Chinese allies had become especially adept at repairing bombed-out roads and constructing bypasses to keep the troops and supplies flowing. It was also an increasingly lethal environment. By 1971, Hanoi had moved eight SAM batteries into Laos to back up its 545 antiaircraft guns already operating there. US interdiction of the

Ho Chi Minh Trail certainly complicated Hanoi's military actions in South Vietnam and Cambodia from 1968 to 1970 but it did not prevent PAVN from ousting the South Vietnamese army from Laos in 1971. And as historian John Sherwood has aptly observed, even after years of enduring US bombing of the trail, "the North Vietnamese were still able to launch the Easter Offensive, a campaign that nearly defeated the Republic of Vietnam."

Tit-for-Tat Operations

After the halt of bombing operations in North Vietnam at the end of October 1968, the incoming Nixon administration concluded that it had an "understanding" with Hanoi allowing unarmed US reconnaissance planes to overfly North Vietnam. That assumption proved false. On November 15, antiaircraft guns shot down an RA-5C Vigilante flying near Vinh. In response, Washington paired fighter aircraft with the recce planes on missions south of the 19th parallel and authorized the former to attack enemy air defenses if fired upon. Navy and Air Force aircrews soon broadened that interpretation to include striking radars that only tracked US aircraft. Fleet combat aircraft would often fly so-called "trolling" missions in the vicinity of a SAM battery, hoping to be fired upon so they could then attack and destroy the site. The Seventh Air Force commander, General John D. Lavelle, was fired, however, for authorizing his units to carry out unauthorized preplanned strikes on such North Vietnamese targets.

Seventh Fleet aviators also had to contend with MiGs that threatened the reconnaissance planes. On March 28, 1970, Lieutenant (jg) Jerome Beaulier and his radar intercept officer, Lieutenant Steven Barkley, shot down a MiG-21 with Sidewinders. In early May, as US and South Vietnamese forces advanced into Cambodia, Nixon authorized a one-time Navy and Air Force strike on logistic targets near the Mu Gia and Ban Karai passes. Surprising the enemy, the air forces pummeled the site, destroying more than 10,000 tons of supplies staged there. Then, in November, when US special forces launched an unsuccessful effort to rescue POWs thought to be in the prison camp at Son Tay, North Vietnam, Seventh Fleet aircraft carried out diversionary attacks near Haiphong.

Throughout this period, Admiral Moorer, then the JCS chairman, pressed the new defense secretary, Melvin Laird, for authority to launch major strike operations against North Vietnam. Laird, who opposed another bombing campaign, routinely shot down those requests but on occasion gave in to Nixon's favorite military officer. In February 1972, for instance, the fleet was given the green light for three days of strikes against SAM sites near Laos. The fleet's

Communications relay ship *Annapolis* (AGMR-1) steams in the South China Sea during the mid-1960s facilitating electronic contact between ships of the fleet and theater-wide shore stations. *Annapolis* normally operated at sea for two months at a time, but periodically put in at Cam Ranh Bay for supplies. (NHHC)

surface warships also entered the fray when guided missile cruiser *Oklahoma City* launched a Talos missile at a radar site near Thanh Hoa. Guided missile destroyer *Sterett* (DLG-31) then teamed up with an Air Force F-4 Phantom flown by Major Robert Lodge and his back-seater, Major Roger Locher, to shoot down a MiG far from the sea over Laos. The ship's Radarman 1st Class William Bunch had warned Lodge of enemy bandits closing on him, enabling the crew to turn the tables on the attacker.

Despite these relatively isolated actions from 1968 to 1972, neither North Vietnam nor the United States gained a serious military advantage from them. The North Vietnamese demonstrated that they would not allow their enemy to fly openly in their skies and the Americans showed that they still had the capability to inflict damage on North Vietnamese air defenses. These were only displays of resolve, not major military campaigns. President Nixon knew full well of Hanoi's intention to launch an invasion of South Vietnam in early 1972. He expected that "surprise" attack to galvanize American and world opinion which would enable him to launch a renewed military campaign against North Vietnam to end the war.

Learning from *Rolling Thunder*

Rolling Thunder did not fail for lack of trying. During the campaign, Navy and Marine aircraft flew 152,399 attack sorties against North Vietnam, close to the Air Force total of 153,784. The two air services released 864,000 tons of bombs and missiles on North Vietnam, which surpassed the totals for the Korean War and World War II in the Pacific theater. During the entire war, enemy action and operational mishaps claimed 1,125 Navy and Marine fixed-wing aircraft and helicopters, the greatest number during *Rolling Thunder*. The Navy suffered the loss of 600 and the Marine Corps 271 aviators, most during that campaign. The Communists captured 170 naval aviators and aircrewmen. Hanoi released 160 of them in 1973. A total of 569 sailors and Marines remain on the rolls of those men who went missing in North and South Vietnam, Laos, Cambodia, China, and at sea and whose remains have not been returned to the United States.

Soon after taking office in January 1969, President Richard M. Nixon, in contrast to his predecessor, set clear objectives in relation to the conflict in Southeast Asia. He planned to withdraw the US armed forces from South Vietnam, prepare the South Vietnamese military to take over the fight, negotiate a lasting peace with Hanoi, and bring home American POWs. He also promised South Vietnamese leaders that they could count on the United States to come to their aid with air and naval support if Hanoi invaded the Republic of Vietnam. Finally, the president was determined to show Moscow and Beijing that even after the war, the United States and its armed forces would remain potent global adversaries. Nixon recognized that since Moscow was keen on signing a nuclear arms control agreement and Beijing was looking to normalize US–PRC relations, he could take direct military action to further US interests in Vietnam.

The Nixon White House gave naval commanders greater latitude in selecting what they considered to be the most effective operations and tactics, aircraft, and weapons for a particular operation or mission. Learning from the *Rolling Thunder* experience, naval leaders planned in future to launch more nighttime two-plane or even one-plane surgical strikes by all-weather A-6 Intruder attack planes as a complement to the multiplane and resource-heavy Alpha strikes. Building on the successful experience with precision-guided munitions during *Rolling Thunder*, the Seventh Fleet and the Air Force stocked up on laser-guided bombs, electro-optical glide bombs, and other "smart" weapons. This ordnance gave the services much greater capability to take out key bridges and other targets that had survived years of pounding or near misses by conventional bombs. After testing in *Rolling Thunder*, the fleet introduced the Standard ARM (AGM-78) anti-radiation missile which was bigger than the Shrike and packed a more powerful warhead. Where Shrikes had been employed against singular radars in a tactical sense, Standard ARMs had the capability to take out enemy radars in a much larger area. When North Vietnamese air defense controllers detected a Standard ARM in the air, they frequently shut down all their radars in the region.

Learning from the combat experience prior to 1972, naval leaders planned to employ more technologically advanced fighter, attack, and reconnaissance aircraft over North Vietnam, where the enemy's air defenses could be expected to be even more sophisticated than they had been. Those first-line aircraft included F-4 Phantoms, A-6 Intruders, A-7 Corsairs, and RA-5Cs. New EA-6B Prowlers

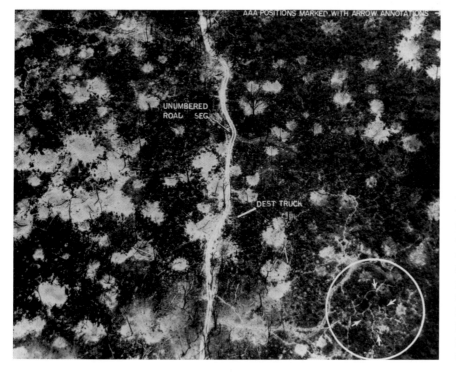

A heavily bombed segment of the Ho Chi Minh Trail photographed by a fleet reconnaissance plane. An enemy antiaircraft position can be seen in the lower right corner of the image. Combat operations in Laos became the focus of Task Force 77 operations from late 1968 to early 1972. (NHHC)

and other electronic countermeasures aircraft would help to limit Navy losses. Indeed, by the end of the war, much improved electronic countermeasures tactics, equipment, and anti-radar weapons had markedly reduced aircraft losses to enemy surface-to-air missiles. The squadrons at Yankee Station were also reinforced with upgraded Sparrow radar-guided missiles and heat-seeking Sidewinders. Seventh Fleet leaders determined that the "old reliables," the A-4 Skyhawks and propeller-driven A-1 Skyraiders, were better suited to the less lethal skies over South Vietnam. Unhappy with the 2 to 1 ratio of Seventh Fleet aerial victories to losses during *Rolling Thunder*, the Navy had established "Top Gun," the Fighter Weapons School, at Naval Air Station Miramar in California. The training focused on preparing naval air crews for air combat at close quarters.

By 1972, the Seventh Fleet's surface warships and their veteran sailors had become especially skilled at putting heavy, accurate fire on North Vietnam's coastal defenses and transportation system and sinking enemy logistics craft heading south. Having learned how to avoid or silence enemy counterbattery fire, the fleet's major warships were prepared in future to steam close to Haiphong and open fire on targets miles inland. They would be protected by an armada of guided missile cruisers and destroyers that could knock down enemy planes far inland or over the fleet with Talos and Terrier surface-to-air missiles. By 1972 the Seventh Fleet had demonstrated that enemy combat vessels venturing out to sea were headed for destruction. And, by 1972, the PIRAZ ships had more than proven their worth in tracking MiGs over North Vietnam and Laos, warning US aircraft of aerial ambushes, and vectoring US fighters to the threat. Veteran sonarmen on board these ships had on numerous occasions demonstrated their technological prowess. The Seventh Fleet had also learned from the tragic personnel and materiel losses suffered during the *Oriskany*, *Forrestal*, and *Enterprise* conflagrations, introducing effective measures for limiting the risk of fire on board carriers.

Guided missile cruiser *Chicago* (CG-11) (foreground), and guided missile destroyer *Sterett* (DLG-31), employed advanced radars and highly trained personnel to help protect Navy and Air Force aircraft flying over North Vietnam and Laos. They also used their surface-to-air missiles to shoot down enemy MiGs that threatened the fleet. (NHHC)

In short, *Rolling Thunder* was a strategic failure but the leaders and sailors of the Seventh Fleet exploited the experience to develop a highly trained, technologically advanced, and combat-ready instrument of US national power. The fleet's enhanced capability and combat performance in 1972 would provide the Nixon administration with a powerful means to achieve its wartime goals.

1972: Fighting to End the War

The Seventh Fleet's opportunity to demonstrate its enhanced ability to project naval power ashore followed North Vietnam's March 30, 1972 Nguyen Hue invasion of South Vietnam (to Americans the Easter Offensive). PAVN forces, reinforced with Soviet-designed T-54 main battle tanks, PT-76 armored fighting vehicles, 130mm long-range artillery, and shoulder-fired SA-7 Strela surface-to-air missiles, crashed across the demilitarized zone between North and South Vietnam. Hanoi's objective was to overrun South Vietnam's Military Region I and the areas north of Saigon and in the country's Central Highlands. The enemy's ultimate goal was to destroy the armed forces of South Vietnam and end the independence of the Republic of Vietnam. North Vietnamese troops quickly overcame South Vietnamese opposition and moved on south toward Quang Tri City and the old imperial capital of Hue. By March 1972, only a small number of US military personnel remained in-country.

President Nixon was determined to honor his pledge to aid America's ally and to demonstrate his resolve to Soviet and Chinese leaders. He ordered the deployment to the Western Pacific of substantial naval and air forces. By May 15, for the first time in the war six aircraft carriers and 95 other warships and support vessels constituted the naval power of the Seventh Fleet. He also gathered on Guam and in Thailand a strategic bomber force of 210 B-52s. Meanwhile, the Seventh Fleet's combat squadrons, cruisers, destroyers, and amphibious units entered the fray. These naval forces would prove instrumental to defeat of the enemy's Nguyen Hue offensive in northern South Vietnam. Heavy clouds and rainfall made flying almost impossible during the first weeks of the attack. Seventh Fleet warships, however, answered the call for naval gunfire support. The destroyers of the Naval Gunfire Support Unit (Task Unit 70.8.9) deployed to the waters off MR I. A quartet of destroyers and later as many as 20 warships bombarded enemy formations trying to move south along the main coastal highway, QL 1. The destroyers' 5in/54-caliber guns could hit targets 12 miles from the sea in this geographically constricted region. Marine advisor Captain John Ripley complimented the destroyers of the task unit for their accurate and timely fire against the enemy's road-bound tanks and armored fighting vehicles. By mid-month, Seventh Fleet surface ships had fired more than 83,000 rounds in support of the South Vietnamese troops. In the third week of April, good weather returned, enabling attack squadrons from *Coral Sea*, *Hancock*, and *Kitty Hawk* to execute 2,000 tactical air strikes in support of the South Vietnamese. PAVN forces seized Quang Tri City on May 1 but then their advance stalled along the My Chanh River just to the south.

TURNING THE TIDE:
AIR AND NAVAL SUPPORT TO GROUND FORCES

Seventh Fleet aircraft carriers, cruisers, destroyers, amphibious ships, and sea-based Marine units mounted a major effort in the spring and summer of 1972 to defeat North Vietnam's Easter Offensive that threatened to overrun South Vietnam's entire Military Region I. At the outset, units of the People's Army of Vietnam (PAVN) equipped with battle tanks, long-range artillery, and shoulder-fired surface-to-air missiles crashed through the DMZ, seized Quang Tri City, and came close to destroying units of the defending Army of Vietnam (ARVN). The Seventh Fleet units that responded to the threat poured fire into the enemy's flank on the South China Sea and along the major north–south highway, QL-1. The fleet's Amphibious Ready Group/Special Landing Force landed South Vietnamese marines behind enemy lines in surprise operations and mounted a number of feint operations to confuse the enemy. That Navy–Marine Corps effort helped the South Vietnamese army hold the line and then mount a counterattack that liberated Quang Tri City in September.

The president decided that since Hanoi had launched the invasion from North Vietnam, that country was now once again fair game for American sea and air power. On April 5, he authorized air and naval attacks against targets in North Vietnam up to the 19th parallel. As part of Operation *Freedom Train*, Seventh Fleet cruisers and destroyers steamed along the enemy coast hitting coastal and air defense sites, bridges, road traffic, and coastal craft. On the 14th, Admiral Moorer authorized the Navy's warships to bombard military targets north of the 20th parallel. The Johnson administration had severely limited the ability of these ships to strike targets on the coast and kept them far south of Haiphong, but Nixon wanted to level the port facilities there. On the 16th, *Oklahoma City* (CLG-5) and four destroyers joined with carrier squadrons to strike Haiphong's petroleum storage facilities and coastal defense sites. By October, Seventh Fleet warships had returned five times to hit targets around Haiphong, expending more than 111,000 rounds and sinking 200 vessels all along the coast. Enemy fire routinely missed the fast-moving warships, but on occasion it registered. On April 19, for instance, an enemy round killed a sailor and wounded seven other crewmen of destroyer *Buchanan*. The enemy's coastal guns, mostly army field artillery pieces, did not sink a single US warship but operational mishaps damaged ships and ended the service life of others. That same month, faulty Navy–Air Force operational procedures resulted in guided missile frigate *Worden* (DLG-18) taking a hit from an Air Force AGM-45 Shrike that killed one sailor and wounded another 13.

To bolster the Seventh Fleet's intelligence capability, Naval Security Group increased from six to 20 its Direct Support Units deployed on board Seventh Fleet combatants. The highly trained and experienced personnel in these units provided friendly forces with timely signals and communications intelligence. The fleet intelligence facility at Cubi Point in the Philippines definitely proved its worth in 1972, developing information to support the air and naval

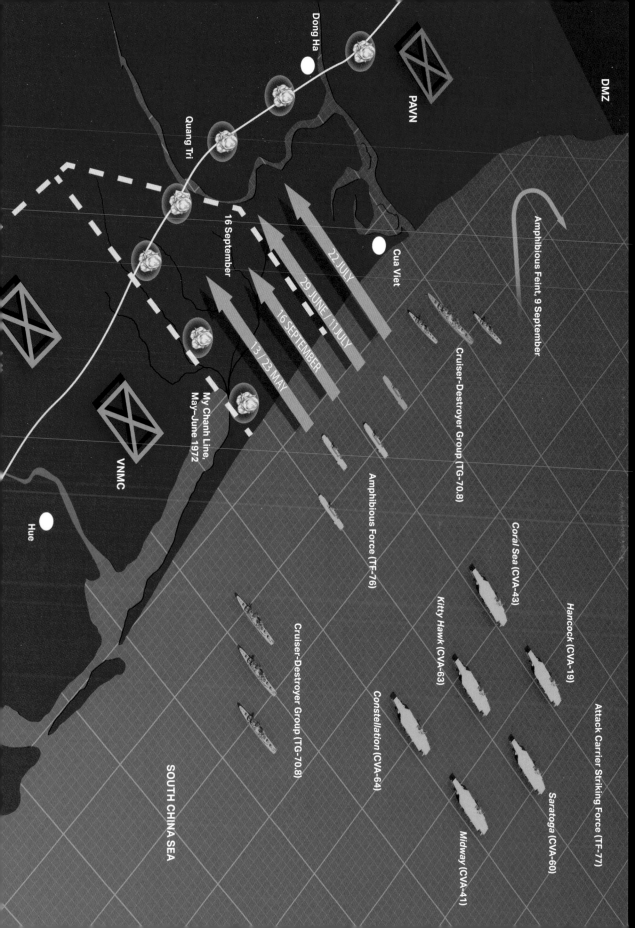

DMZ

Dong Ha

PAVN

Quang Tri

16 September

22 JULY

29 JUNE / 11 JULY

16 SEPTEMBER

13 / 23 MAY

Cua Viet

Amphibious Feint, 9 September

Cruiser-Destroyer Group (TG-70.8)

Amphibious Force (TF-76)

Coral Sea (CVA-43)

Hancock (CVA-19)

Kitty Hawk (CVA-63)

Attack Carrier Striking Force (TF-77)

Constellation (CVA-64)

Saratoga (CVA-60)

Midway (CVA-41)

My Chanh Line,
May–June 1972

VNMC

Cruiser-Destroyer Group (TG-70.8)

Hue

SOUTH CHINA SEA

bombardment operations against North Vietnam. The facility also provided up-to-date information on the enemy's antiaircraft guns, SAM batteries, bridges, fuel storage facilities, and rail lines. FICPACFAC's *Linebacker* Analysis Group produced weekly reports on the results of air interdiction operations and potential targets for bombardment. The command also provided the fleet's naval gunfire ships with the latest information on enemy coastal defense sites.

Taking advantage of the fleet's increasing ability to operate in the coastal waters of North Vietnam, submarine *Grayback* took part in a super-secret operation in early June whose aim was to retrieve American POWs who might escape from captivity in North Vietnam. An embarked special operations team of SEAL and Underwater Demolition Team personnel, led by Lieutenant M. Spence Dry, intended to set up observation points with the use of swimmer delivery vehicles (SDVs) off the mouth of the Red River and there await any escapees. Even though *Grayback* maintained a periscope vigil offshore, the SDVs proved ill-suited for the mission. At one point, a CSAR helicopter dropped members of the team into the sea atop what was mistakenly thought to be the submarine's beacon. The drop killed Lieutenant Dry, the last SEAL to die in the war, and badly injured another man. While an unsuccessful mission, it demonstrated the determination of the CSAR forces to save fellow Americans. During 1972, Navy, Air Force, Army, Marine, and South Vietnamese aircraft and Seventh Fleet ships rescued 261 aircrewmen.

In July, destroyer *Warrington* struck what turned out to be an errant US Destructor mine. The damage was so severe that the ship had to be stricken from the Navy list. In October, an even greater calamity befell heavy cruiser *Newport News* (CA-148) when an explosion in one of the 8in gun mounts killed 19 sailors and wounded 36 men. Combat took the lives of another 32 battleship, cruiser, destroyer, and destroyer escort sailors during the war. A further 32 naval

An accidental explosion in turret number two of heavy cruiser *Newport News* (CA-148), a mainstay of the fleet's bombardment and naval gunfire support force, killed or wounded 55 sailors. Operational accidents at sea could often be just as deadly as combat. (NHHC)

personnel, including Rear Admiral Rembrandt C. Robinson, lost their lives or went missing as a result of turret explosions or other operational mishaps. The 1969 collision in the South China Sea involving destroyer *Frank E. Evans* (DD-754) and carrier HMAS *Melbourne* resulted in the death of 74 American sailors.

Enemy air attacks on the fleet were rare but on April 19, two now obsolete MiG-17s flew against a task unit near Dong Hoi. One of the jets dropped a 550lb bomb on the aft gun of destroyer *Higbee* (DD-806) that leveled the unoccupied turret and injured four sailors nearby. For that dubious accomplishment, the North Vietnamese paid with the loss of a MiG to a Terrier surface-to-air missile fired by guided missile destroyer *Sterett*. Easily withstanding an attack by five MiGs in July, *Biddle* (DLG-34) shot down two of the aggressors. Navy and Air Force fighter squadrons also took a toll of enemy fighters, shooting down eight MiGs during the first four months of 1972 without suffering a loss.

On August 27, 1972, Hanoi sent three Soviet-made P-6 torpedo boats out at night to sink a Seventh Fleet cruiser-destroyer task unit that had just bombarded targets around Haiphong. A pair of A-6 Intruders, and perhaps naval gunfire, sent two of the attackers to the bottom. Despite years of pleading by the North Vietnamese, only in the last weeks of the war did Moscow provide its Asian ally with Komar-class missile boats armed with SS-N-2 Styx anti-ship missiles. Aircraft from *Enterprise* promptly sank one of the four boats that they found trying to hide among the rocks in Ha Long Bay.

While Task Force 77 concentrated its efforts on North Vietnam, other Seventh Fleet contingents continued helping the South Vietnamese army fight off the enemy onslaught in MR I. Marine helicopters of Task Force 76 operating from amphibious assault ship *Okinawa* (LPH-3) airlifted South Vietnamese marines behind enemy lines near Quang Tri City. Landing craft from other amphibious ships put more South Vietnamese marines on the beach. In May, June, and July, the allied amphibious forces carried out five major operations and several feints to confuse enemy defenders. In July, dock landing ship *Alamo* (LSD-33) emplaced a causeway on the beach east of Quang Tri that the South Vietnamese used for ammunition resupply. Assisted by allied sea and air power, which inflicted 80 percent of the enemy's casualties, in September South Vietnamese marine and airborne troops liberated Quang Tri City. By the end of the war, South Vietnamese forces had secured the fighting front just south of the DMZ.

The Seventh Fleet employed against the enemy another naval warfare asset, mine warfare. Between 0859 and 0901 on 9 May, six Navy A-7 Corsairs and three Marine A-6 Intruders flying from *Coral Sea* dropped 36 Mk-52 magnetic sea mines in the water approaches to Haiphong. The surprise Operation *Pocket Money* closed North Vietnam's major port for the rest of the war. In short order, and without casualties, the fleet had accomplished a task that Washington had failed to order since the beginning of the conflict. In later months, fleet aircraft dropped 11,700 more Mk-52 and Mk-36 Destructors in North Vietnam's coastal and inland waterways. *Pocket Money* severely impacted Hanoi's ability to

MINING OF HAIPHONG, 1972

The Seventh Fleet demonstrated its unique capability to deny an enemy nation's access to outside military and economic support – another facet of the fleet's capability for offensive warfare – when on May 9, 1972 it mined and closed the port of Haiphong, through which had passed 85 percent of North Vietnam's overseas trade. The quick and casualty-free operation complicated Hanoi's war effort and helped end US involvement in the conflict. The operation was carried out by aircraft from two Navy and one Marine attack squadron flying from aircraft carrier *Coral Sea* (CVA-43). A trio of A-6A Intruders and six A-7E Corsairs seeded the approaches to Haiphong with 36 Mk-52 magnetic sea mines and later Mk-36 Destructors. Without the enemy's knowledge, the fleet's mine warfare experts programmed the weapons to self-destruct or knew when they would cease to function. The mining operation closed the port for the duration of the war. The depiction identifies the attack squadrons involved and shows the path of the Navy and Marine planes dropping the mines in the channel approaches to Haiphong. It identifies the destroyers that shelled enemy antiaircraft defenses on the nearby Do Son Peninsula, and the cruiser-destroyer group that shot down one MiG heading for the minelayers and compelled the other two to abort their mission; and shows the paths of the three North Vietnamese SA-2 surface-to-air missiles that fired at but failed to hit the minelayers.

receive supplies of SA-2 surface-to-air missiles, limiting means of import to the heavily bombed rail and road links from China. Imports from China to North Vietnam during *Linebacker* fell from 160,000 tons a month to just 30,000 tons.

As an example of the fleet's offensive confidence in 1972, on the first day of *Pocket Money* guided missile cruiser *Chicago*, operating 30 miles southeast of Haiphong on a missile defense line with *Long Beach* and *Sterett*, used a Talos missile to shoot down one of three MiGs heading for the mining planes and scared off the other two. In addition, that same morning destroyers *Buchanan* (DDG-14), *Richard S. Edwards* (DD-950), and *Myles C. Fox* (DD-829) carried out a diversionary bombardment on the nearby Do Son Peninsula. A North Vietnamese account related that during this period, the Seventh Fleet's "shelling attacks inflicted serious losses on us without receiving any punishment whatsoever."

Task Force 77 hit the enemy with even more devastating firepower on May 10, the first day of the *Linebacker* campaign. The goal of the campaign was to limit North Vietnam's war-making capability. Three times that day, in league with Air Force attacks around Hanoi, multiplane strikes from *Coral Sea*, *Kitty Hawk*, and *Constellation* smashed bridge, rail, road, and other targets around Haiphong, Hai Duong, and Hon Gai/Cam Pha. As a reflex action, North Vietnam's leaders ordered their MiG force to rise and fight the American air forces; it was a huge mistake. In little more than five minutes, Seventh Fleet F-4 Phantoms shot down six of the 11 enemy MiGs that Navy and Air Force fighters claimed that day. On May 10, F-4 pilot Lieutenant Randy Cunningham and his radar intercept officer, Lieutenant (jg) William Driscoll, both trained at "Top Gun," became the war's first aces. They achieved the last of their five wartime aerial victories. May turned out to be the worst month of the war for the MiG-17s of North Vietnam's 923rd Fighter Regiment. Moreover, in 1972 the carrier squadrons registered a thirteen-to-one victory to loss ratio.

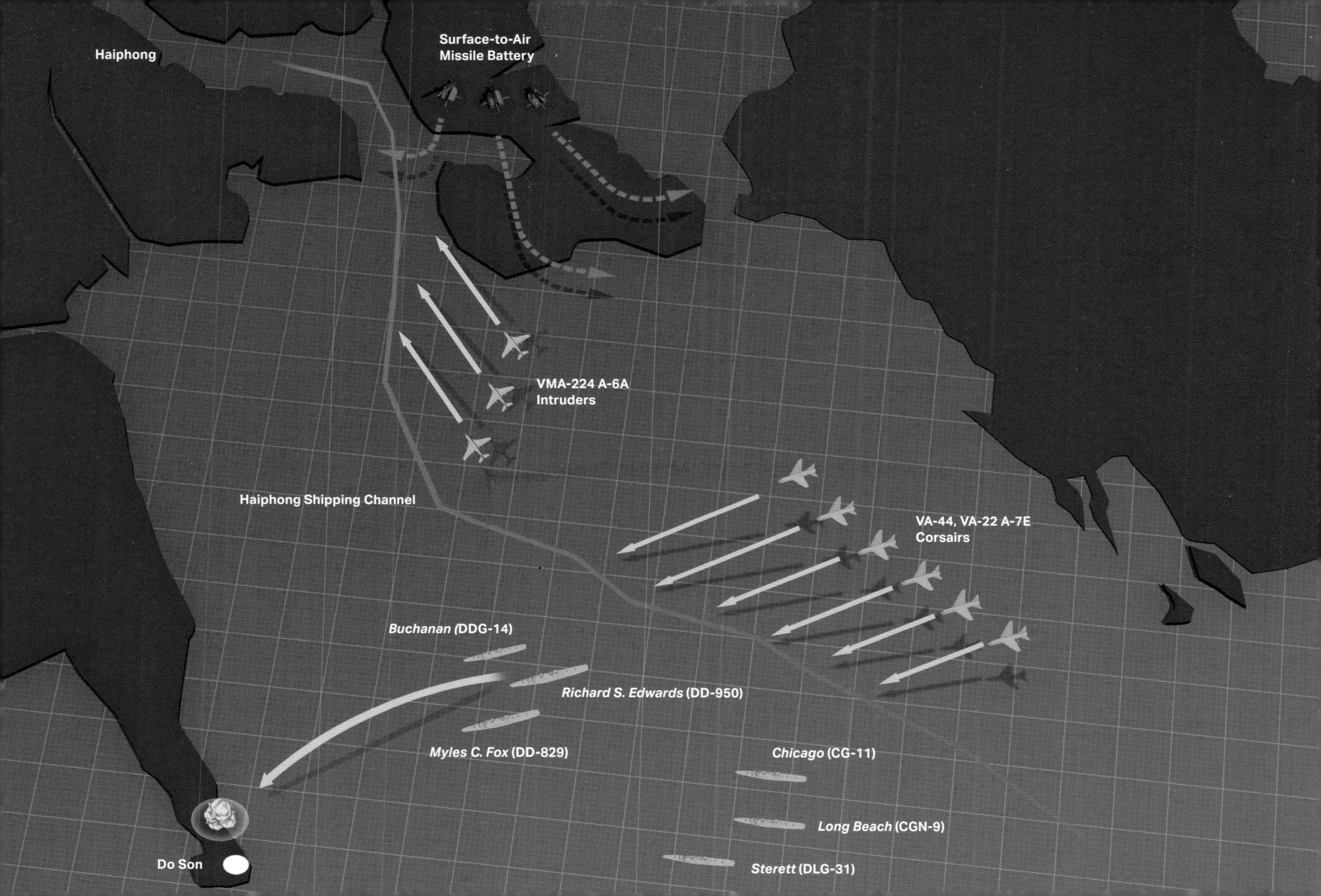

Haiphong

Do Son

Haiphong Shipping Channel

Surface-to-Air
Missile Battery

VMA-224 A-6A
Intruders

Buchanan (DDG-14)

Myles C. Fox (DD-829)

Richard S. Edwards (DD-950)

Chicago (CG-11)

Long Beach (CGN-9)

Sterett (DLG-31)

VA-44, VA-22 A-7E
Corsairs

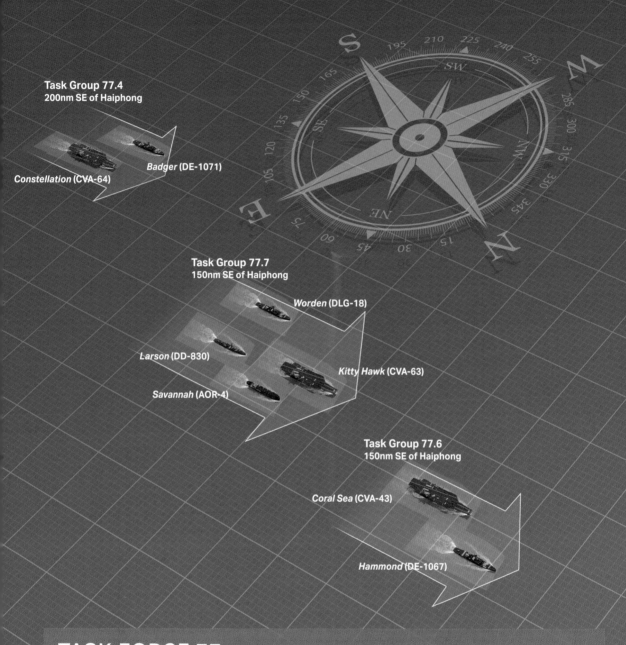

Task Group 77.4
200nm SE of Haiphong

Badger (DE-1071)

Constellation (CVA-64)

Task Group 77.7
150nm SE of Haiphong

Worden (DLG-18)

Larson (DD-830)

Kitty Hawk (CVA-63)

Savannah (AOR-4)

Task Group 77.6
150nm SE of Haiphong

Coral Sea (CVA-43)

Hammond (DE-1067)

TASK FORCE 77
LINEBACKER DEPLOYMENT, MAY 10, 1972

Carrier escort ships routinely operated at a point station with a fixed bearing and range to the carrier or in a sector screen station in perhaps a 60-degree arc from the carrier. The escorts normally operated 4,000 to 6,000 yards from the carrier. To conduct engineering drills or helicopter support operations, sometimes at night, the escort ships often steamed independently of the carrier while maintaining visual or radio contact. Carrier escorts on occasion detached from the carrier screen to drive off Soviet AGIs that attempted to monitor carrier flight

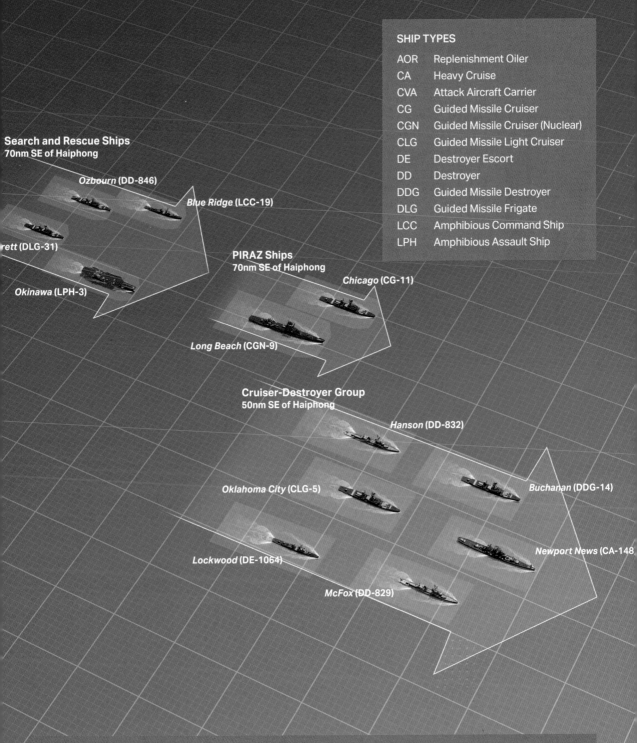

SHIP TYPES

AOR	Replenishment Oiler
CA	Heavy Cruise
CVA	Attack Aircraft Carrier
CG	Guided Missile Cruiser
CGN	Guided Missile Cruiser (Nuclear)
CLG	Guided Missile Light Cruiser
DE	Destroyer Escort
DD	Destroyer
DDG	Guided Missile Destroyer
DLG	Guided Missile Frigate
LCC	Amphibious Command Ship
LPH	Amphibious Assault Ship

Search and Rescue Ships
70nm SE of Haiphong

Ozbourn (DD-846)

Blue Ridge (LCC-19)

rett (DLG-31)

Okinawa (LPH-3)

PIRAZ Ships
70nm SE of Haiphong

Chicago (CG-11)

Long Beach (CGN-9)

Cruiser-Destroyer Group
50nm SE of Haiphong

Hanson (DD-832)

Oklahoma City (CLG-5)

Buchanan (DDG-14)

Lockwood (DE-1064)

Newport News (CA-148

McFox (DD-829)

operations and report that information to their North Vietnamese allies.

During flight operations, escorts served as "plane guards" positioned 1,500 to 4,000 yards astern of the carrier ready to pick up aviators forced to eject from their aircraft.

When an oiler or ammunition ship rendezvoused with a carrier for underway replenishment, an escort ship typically did the same while steaming on the starboard side of the support ship. An escort might also operate 1,500 yards astern of the UNREP ship to rescue any sailor lost overboard during resupply operations.

Even more than in previous years, the highly trained air intercept controllers and other key personnel serving on board the guided missile cruisers posted to the PIRAZ station southeast of Haiphong earned renown. As one example of their exceptional technical skill and situational awareness, *Chicago's* Senior Chief Radarman Larry Nowell took part in more than 1,500 aerial intercepts and earned a Navy Distinguished Service Medal for helping Navy and Air Force fighters shoot down 12 MiGs.

The AGM-52 Walleye TV-guided bomb, first tested in combat during *Rolling Thunder*, proved to be a significant bridge-buster during *Linebacker*. Walleyes and Air Force laser-guided bombs destroyed almost all of North Vietnam's major rail and highway bridges, especially those between Hanoi and Haiphong and the border with China. Walleyes also took out the enemy's key bridges in the southern panhandle. On October 6, for instance, A-7E Corsairs of Attack Squadron 82 hit the Thanh Hoa (Dragon's Jaw) bridge, notorious for surviving numerous strikes by the US air forces during *Rolling Thunder*. On this occasion, however, the aircraft piloted by Commander (later four-star admiral) Leighton "Snuffy" Smith and his wingman, Lieutenant (jg) Marvin Baldwin, along with two other A-7s, severed the bridge with two Walleyes and conventional munitions. Follow-on missions kept the structure inoperable for the rest of the war. By the late summer of 1972, Task Force 77 aircraft were conducting 4,700 *Linebacker* attack sorties every month.

Secretary of State Henry Kissinger, negotiating with North Vietnamese diplomats in Paris, suggested in October that "peace is at hand." It was not to be. The belligerents could not agree on the terms of a ceasefire. As a result, Nixon decided after he had won the presidential election in November that he would unleash the US bomber fleet and the tactical combat squadrons of Task Force 77 and the Air Force in a massive aerial assault on North Vietnam. The strategic goal was to inflict maximum damage on Hanoi's war-making capability and convince the leaders in Hanoi of Nixon's determination to end the war by any means.

With the kick-off of the *Linebacker II* campaign on December 18, waves of B-52s smashed targets close to the capital as the combat squadrons flying from *Midway*, *America*, and *Ranger* concentrated their strikes on Haiphong. Seventh Fleet cruisers and destroyers joined in with the round-the-clock bombardment of targets along the coast. On December 28, following a massive B-52 bombing raid on Hanoi, North Vietnam's leaders finally agreed to meet to end the war. That gathering produced the Paris Agreement of January 27, 1973.

In conclusion, the sea and air power of the Seventh Fleet proved instrumental to the US-South Vietnamese defeat of North Vietnam's Nguyen Hue Offensive and to the strategic effort to compel Hanoi to end the war. US sea power enabled Nixon to aid South Vietnam's fight for survival. It also facilitated the president's desire to convince Moscow and Beijing of continued US military power and relevance in the Cold War world. The Seventh Fleet made significant operational contributions to allied success during 1972. Navy and the Air Force bombing operations proved critical to defeat of the enemy's offensive in South

Vietnam, seriously damaged North Vietnam's air and coastal defenses, and leveled heavy military and psychological pressure on enemy leaders to stop the war. The fleet's mining campaign cut off North Vietnam from seaborne supply, interdicted the flow of coastal traffic, and reduced Hanoi's access to supplies from China to the rail lines and roads north of Hanoi and Haiphong. The fleet's cruiser-destroyer, amphibious, and carrier forces helped South Vietnamese military forces frustrate the enemy advance on Hue and then launch an allied counterattack that liberated Quang Tri City. The fleet's major warships also put heavy pressure on the enemy's logistical infrastructure in southern North Vietnam and around Haiphong. Fleet aircraft and surface ships neutralized North Vietnam's navy by sinking or damaging its torpedo boats and gunboats at sea, along the coast, and in port. In short, as Admiral Moorer, the JCS chairman and former Commander Seventh Fleet, observed, air and sea power "given its day in court after almost a decade of frustration, confirmed its effectiveness as an instrument of national power."

AFTERMATH
Final Missions

As a result of the Paris Peace Accords of January 27, 1973, expectations were high in the United States that the war would finally be over. Between February 12 and March 29, 591 American POWs, the majority Air Force and Navy aircrewmen, boarded US planes at Gia Lam airport in Hanoi for the return to their country and their loved ones. With the release of the POWs and the end of hostilities in North Vietnam, one would have thought that the Seventh Fleet had carried out its last operations of the conflict, but it was not to be. One day after the signing of the Paris agreement, attack squadrons from *Constellation*

THE SURFACE FLEET IN THE LION'S DEN (overleaf)

After bombarding Cat Bi airfield and other targets in North Vietnam near Haiphong in Operation *Lion's Den* on August 27, 1972, Seventh Fleet heavy cruiser *Newport News* (CA-148), destroyer *Rowan* (DD-782), light cruiser *Providence* (CLG-6), and guided missile destroyer *Robison* (DDG-12) headed for the deeper waters of the Gulf of Tonkin. The 8in and 5in guns of *Newport News* and *Rowan* are depicted firing on North Vietnamese Soviet-made P-6 torpedo boats to the east. These boats used the rocky outcroppings near Bach Long Vi island to confuse US surface ships' search and fire-control radars.

Rockeye cluster bombs dropped by a Seventh Fleet A-7 attack aircraft have heavily damaged an enemy boat, illuminated by flares deployed by a second American Corsair. Rockeye bombs and gunfire from the surface warships eventually sank two of the three attackers (T-319 and T-349). Throughout the war, Seventh Fleet ships ranged the coast of North Vietnam bombarding bridges, railways, and supply caches ashore, and together with carrier aircraft, neutralized the North Vietnamese navy by sinking its combat craft and logistic vessels in port, along the coast, and out to sea.

and *Oriskany* launched strikes against targets on the Ho Chi Minh Trail. For the next 28 months the North Vietnamese and their Communist allies continued to seek the destruction of the governments and armed forces of Laos, Cambodia, and South Vietnam which the administrations of Richard Nixon and Gerald R. Ford energetically but unsuccessfully worked to prevent.

Early in the new year, Seventh Fleet forces once more operated in the Gulf of Tonkin to carry out a special mission. As called for in the Paris agreement, the fleet was tasked with ensuring that all the mines laid in the waters of North Vietnam during the war would no longer pose a threat to shipping. In Operation *End Sweep*, Rear Admiral Brian McCauley's Mine Countermeasures Force (Task Force 78) deployed off Haiphong. His ocean minesweepers, protected by a force of guided missile and conventional destroyers, began their mine countermeasures work on February 27. Complementing the mine countermeasures ships were 31 CH-53 Sea Stallion helicopters of the Navy's Helicopter Mine Countermeasures Squadron 12 and the Marine Corps' helicopter squadrons HMM-165 and HMH-463. The aircraft employed minesweeping sleds and other equipment to carry out the aerial minesweeping of North Vietnam's shallow port areas and inland waterways. In addition to Haiphong, the task force focused their efforts on the shipping channels to the ports of Hon Gai and Cam Pha. In early April, McCauley dispatched MSS-2, an old, decommissioned LST filled with foam and crewed by a small number of volunteer sailors up the Haiphong channel in eight check runs to convince the North Vietnamese that no mines remained to threaten their oceangoing trade. Even though the Americans knew that the mines had been set to deactivate soon after their deployment or had self-destructed, Hanoi demanded reassurance.

In July, finally, the admiral declared that the water approaches to Haiphong, Hon Gai, and Cam Pha and coastal waters to the south were free of mines. Having completed its Operation *End Sweep* mission, the Seventh Fleet task force steamed for the open sea, gladly leaving North Vietnam in its wake.

The Seventh Fleet once again concentrated off Indochina on the eve of the conquest of Cambodia by Khmer Rouge Communist forces. Operation *Eagle Pull*'s mission was to rescue American and threatened allied personnel from the capital, Phnom Penh. By April 12, Amphibious Ready Group Alpha and the 31st Marine Amphibious Unit had gathered off Kompong Som (formerly Sihanoukville) in the Gulf of Thailand. On that day, President Ford authorized the evacuation. The Marine contingent loaded 275 evacuees,

In Operation *End Sweep*, a Marine CH-53 Sea Stallion helicopter tows a Mk-105 minesweeping sled (not visible) through the waters of Ha Long Bay and the maritime approaches to Haiphong. In this last major Seventh Fleet operation in the Gulf of Tonkin after the war, the Mine Countermeasures Force (Task Force 78) confirmed North Vietnam's waters clear of all US mines laid during the war. (NHHC)

including US Ambassador John Gunther Dean, embassy staff members, Cambodian officials and their families, and journalists on the Marine helicopters. By early afternoon, all helicopters, evacuees, and military personnel had reached the safety of the Seventh Fleet amphibious group.

Vice Admiral George P. Steele, the Seventh Fleet commander, then turned his attention to preparing his command for the expected withdrawal of all American military and civilian personnel and many Vietnamese from South Vietnam. Earlier, he had deployed the transport ships, barges, and other vessels of the Navy's Military Sealift Command (MSC) off the port of Vung Tau southeast of Saigon. The admiral also concentrated there the fleet's Amphibious Task Force (Task Force 76), under Rear Admiral Donald Whitmire, which consisted of command ship *Blue Ridge* (LCC-19) and 14 amphibious ships. Also on hand was the 9th Marine Amphibious Brigade with three battalion landing teams and four helicopter squadrons. Joining Task Force 76 were the fleet flagship, *Oklahoma City*, eight destroyer types, and aircraft carriers *Hancock* and *Midway*, the latter two ships carrying Marine and Air Force helicopters. *Enterprise* and *Coral Sea*, with a full complement of fighter and attack aircraft, operated further out to sea ready to provide air cover for the mission.

On the 29th, as the enemy closed in on Saigon, President Ford ordered the execution of Operation *Frequent Wind*, the evacuation of Saigon. In the early afternoon, *Hancock* launched the first wave of helicopters that landed at the US Defense Attaché compound in the city. The Task Force 76 helicopters lifted out American, Vietnamese, and third-country nationals, 5,000 by 2100hrs. Two Marines had already been killed at the compound by enemy artillery rounds. Later in the operation, two helicopters and their crews went down in the South China Sea. The Task Force 76 helicopters flew all night, on occasion under fire from the ground, to transport evacuees from another landing zone at the US embassy. By 0500hrs on April 30, US Ambassador Graham Martin and the last of the evacuees had been lifted out of Saigon. Ultimately, Task Force 76 evacuated more than 7,000 Americans and Vietnamese. The Seventh Fleet departed the coast of South Vietnam on the afternoon of April 30 and at dusk

Amphibious assault ship *Okinawa* (LPH-3) steams in the Gulf of Thailand loaded with Marine CH-53 helicopters. In Operation *Eagle Pull* these helicopters and those from aircraft carrier *Hancock* carried out 99 casualty-free missions to evacuate American, Cambodian, and other nationals from Phnom Penh. (NHHC)

Nuclear-powered aircraft carrier *Enterprise* and the carrier's combat aircraft, including new F-14 Tomcat fighters, were on hand off South Vietnam during Operation *Frequent Wind* to ensure the safety from North Vietnamese attack of the Seventh Fleet and Military Sealift Command ships evacuating tens of thousands of people fleeing Indochina in this last act of the Vietnam War. (NHHC)

on May 2 the amphibious task force and the MSC group, with 44,000 refugees embarked, steered a course for the Philippines as did a Vietnam Navy flotilla carrying 30,000 sailors and their families.

The Seventh Fleet was called on once more to employ its combat power in service to US strategic interests and foreign policy in Southeast Asia. On May 12, Khmer Rouge forces seized US merchant ship *Mayaguez* and the crew off Cambodia. P-3 Orions from Patrol Squadron 17, based at Cubi Point in the Philippines, discovered the ship dead in the water with two Cambodian gunboats alongside. The whereabouts of the ship and the crew then became a mystery with the port of Kompong Som and Koh Tang, an island in the Gulf of Thailand, considered possibilities. Soon after, destroyer escort *Harold E. Holt* (DE-1074) came upon *Mayaguez*, abandoned by the Cambodians, and a boarding party of Marines and sailors took control of the ship. Meanwhile, a contingent of 289 Marines, deployed by Air Force helicopters and under heavy fire, had landed on Koh Tang. Guided missile destroyer *Henry B. Wilson* (DDG-7) was on hand to provide the Marines ashore with much-needed naval gunfire support. The *Mayaguez* crewmen were not found on the island and it was later discovered that they had been held briefly in Cambodia and then sent out to sea on a boat to be recovered by the Americans. Determined to impress the Khmer Rouge leaders with his resolve during the crisis, President Ford ordered a strike by *Coral Sea* aircraft on Cambodia's Ream airfield at Kompong Som. The attacking A-7 Corsairs and A-6 Intruders dropped Mk-20 Rockeye cluster bombs and Mk-82 500lb bombs that cratered the runway, destroyed several buildings, and sank a Cambodian river patrol boat. Meanwhile, Air Force helicopters withdrew the Marine contingent from Koh Tang. *Mayaguez* and the ship's crew had been recovered, but at great cost to the US armed forces. Seventy Marine and Air Force personnel had been killed or wounded in the fight and most of the aircraft involved had been destroyed or heavily damaged. Three Marines inadvertently left behind on the island were captured and executed by the Khmer Rouge guerrillas. But America's involvement in the long, bloody conflict in Southeast Asia was finally over.

Appropriately, the power of the US Seventh Fleet, represented in this crisis by *Coral Sea*, *Henry B. Wilson*, and *Harold E. Holt*, had once again been on hand to serve US national security interests in Southeast Asia.

FURTHER READING

Bruhn, David D., *On the Gunline: US Navy and Royal Australian Navy Warships off Vietnam, 1965–1973* (Berwyn Heights, MD, Heritage Books, 2019)

Ethell, Jeffrey, and Alfred Price, *One Day in a Long War: A True Minute-by-Minute Account of Air Combat in Vietnam – Told by the People Who Lived It* (New York, Berkley Books, 1989)

Hanyok, Robert J., *Spartans in Darkness: American SIGINT and the Indochina War, 1945–1975* (Washington, National Security Agency, 2007)

Holloway III, James L., *Aircraft Carriers at War: A Personal Retrospective of Korea, Vietnam, and the Soviet Confrontation* (Annapolis, Naval Institute Press, 2007)

Levinson, Jeffrey L., *Alpha Strike Vietnam: The Navy's Air War, 1964–1973* (Novato, CA, Presidio Press, 1989)

Marolda, Edward J., *Admirals Under Fire: The US Navy and the Vietnam War* (Lubbock, TX, Texas Tech University Press, 2021)

Marolda, Edward J., ed., *Combat at Close Quarters: An Illustrated History of the US Navy in the Vietnam War* (Annapolis, Naval Institute Press, 2018)

Marolda, Edward J., and Oscar P. Fitzgerald, *From Military Assistance to Combat, 1959–1965*, Vol. II in series The United States Navy and the Vietnam Conflict (Washington, Naval Historical Center, 1986)

Marolda, Edward J., ed., *Operation End Sweep: A History of Minesweeping Operations in North Vietnam* (Washington, Naval Historical Center/Tensor Industries, Inc., 1993)

Marolda, Edward J., *Ready Seapower: A History of the US Seventh Fleet* (Washington, Naval History and Heritage Command, 2012)

Marolda, Edward J., *By Sea, Air, and Land: An Illustrated History of the US Navy and the War in Southeast Asia* (Washington, Naval Historical Center, 1994)

Melson, Charles D., and Curtis G. Arnold, *The War That Would Not End, 1971–1973*, US Marines in Vietnam series (Washington, HQUSMC, 1991)

The Military History Institute of Vietnam, *Victory in Vietnam: The Official History of the People's Army of Vietnam, 1954–1975* (Lawrence, KS, University Press of Kansas, 2002)

Moise, Edwin E., *Tonkin Gulf and the Escalation of the Vietnam War* (Annapolis, Naval Institute Press, 2019)

Nichols, John B., and Barrett Tillman, *On Yankee Station: The Naval Air War Over Vietnam* (Annapolis, MD, Naval Institute Press, 2001)

Pribbenow II, Merle L., "The -Ology War: Technology and Ideology in the Vietnamese Defense of Hanoi," *Journal of Military History* (Jan 2003)

Sharp, U. S. G., *Strategy for Defeat* (Novato, CA, Presidio Press, 1978)

Thompson, Wayne, *To Hanoi and Back: The US Air Force and North Vietnam* (Washington, Smithsonian Institution Press, 2000)

Whitcomb, Darrell D., *Moral Imperative: 1972, Combat Rescue, and the End of America's War in Vietnam* (Lawrence, KS, University Press of Kansas, 2021)

INDEX

Note: Page references in **bold** refer to an illustration